SPIRITUAL STEPS TO CHRISTMAS

SPIRITUAL STEPS TO CHRISTMAS

Daily Meditations for Sanctifying Advent

Msgr. Aloysius F. Coogan

TAN Books
Gastonia, North Carolina

Typesetting and revisions in *Spiritual Steps to Christmas: Daily Meditations for Sanctifying Advent* © 2022 TAN Books

All rights reserved. With the exception of short excerpts used in critical review, no part of this work may be reproduced, transmitted, or stored in any form whatsoever, without the prior written permission of the publisher. Creation, exploitation and distribution of any unauthorized editions of this work, in any format in existence now or in the future—including but not limited to text, audio, and video—is prohibited without the prior written permission of the publisher.

Originally published in 1953 by Bruce Publishing, Milwaukee, Wisconsin.

Nihil Obstat:

> *John M. A. Fearns, S.T.D.*
> *Censor librorum*

Imprimatur:

> ✠ *Francis Cardinal Spellman*
> *Archbishop of New York*

August 22, 1953

The nihil obstat and imprimatur are official declarations that a book or pamphlet is free of doctrinal or moral error. No implication is contained therein that those who have granted the nihil obstat and imprimatur agree with the contents, opinions, or statements expressed.

Cover design by Andrew Schmalen

ISBN: 978-1-5051-2836-9
Kindle ISBN: 978-1-5051-2838-3
ePUB ISBN: 978-1-5051-2837-6

Published in the United States by
TAN Books
PO Box 269
Gastonia, NC 28053
www.TANBooks.com

Printed in the United States of America

PRESENTED TO

_____

NAME

_____

DATE / OCCASION

PERSONAL NOTE

_____

_____

_____

_____

_____

_____

_____

Dedicated to the Holy Family, Jesus, Mary, and Joseph, and to my own family, father, mother, sisters, brothers, who, under God, have taught me the true meaning of Christmas.

May the peace of Christ and the joys of the Christmas season dwell in families and hearts, that our homes may be more fruitful nurseries for vocations, and that Priests, Brothers, and Sisters may increase in the family of the Lord to insure the peace of Jesus Christ in the family of nations.

Then shall our Christmas have a real meaning and be a happy, blessed, and merry Christmas.

The Author
Feast of the Sacred Heart
June 12, 1953

CONTENTS

The Christmas Season

PREFACE

The theme of this book suggests that man has gotten away from the true nature of Christmas.

Today, Christmas is celebrated without Christ in many quarters.

Christmas means Christ's Mass. But the Protestant revolt has denied the true sacrifice of the Mass. It has uprooted His altar and replaced it with a pulpit. There are some who profess to be ministers of Christ and yet deny His divinity.

The Real Presence of Christ in the Blessed Sacrament has been removed from their altars and the voice of man has usurped His place. The pivot and focal point of the Protestant Church is not the altar but the pulpit. Man's presence has replaced God's presence; private interpretation has taken the place of God's authority.

Christ is sacrificed in the Mass and the Mass is Christ present with us. Take away the tabernacle of God and, since nature abhors a vacuum, the pulpit of man is ushered in to replace it. Remove the Mass, where Christ is offered and adored, and the result is that man is dehumanized whereas he should be super-naturalized. Man exalts himself instead of humbling himself and adoring God. Without God, man is not even himself. He is dehumanized. He is less than man. For man, as God made him, is just "a little less than the angels."[1] Indeed, since the Immaculate Conception, the highest creature in the universe is a member of our own human race, who God chose as the means to give the Christ His human nature.

And yet, even though Christmas is the season when we celebrate God joining mankind in the form of a child, in how many homes, because Christ is uninvited, children, too, unhappily, are no longer welcome. Christmas, like *Emmanuel*, means "God with us." If we celebrate Christmas without God, we have lost its meaning. If we refuse an inn to God's children as the fruit of marriage, we repeat the sad tale of Bethlehem that refused an inn to Mary and Joseph and the Child. We too deny welcoming Christ into our homes, into our lives, missing the nature of Christmas.

Christmas today, for the average worldling, means nothing more than feasting and food—a holiday, with tinsel and tree, and an exchange of gifts. It is externalized and made pagan in its concept.

---

[1]   Psalm 8:6.

Christmas should, as it is intended to, mean attendance at Mass—at Christ's Mass on Christmas day. It should be a day of great dignity, of rejoicing, as evidenced in a temperate use of food and drink and a meeting of loved ones under the star and spirit of Bethlehem. It should mean not so much a receiving as a giving to Christ's poor in imitation of God who gave Himself to the poor in the greatest of all gifts—His only-begotten Son.

This book is written with the hope and intention of bringing to our minds the thoughts of Advent that we may think and pray with Mary who brought Christ to us. Advent, like Lent, is a time of preparation in thought and deed for a great event. Certainly, if a king or a cardinal were to come to our home as a guest, we would prepare for his advent. Should we not prepare, then, for the great King of the universe during these days? Instead of coming to our homes, however, His Advent, or "coming," is one into our hearts, and it depends on how we pray and meditate during these preparatory days leading up to Christmas.

In thinking of Christmas, we always conjure up in our mind's eye the happy days of childhood, the memory of our parents who may have passed on to their eternal reward, and of our early home—all these are most joyous recollections. Certainly Advent should not be observed in a lugubrious or melancholy manner. Penance is a joy when it is performed for God; when imposed upon us for a selfish motive, it is a drudgery.

These Advent days, then, can be—rather, should be—most joyful, our recollection of former years can be most happy if we dedicate them to God. In simple terms, we can be happiest when all things are in harmony and in their proper place. This is the definition of health. This is the understanding of peace. This is the "tranquility of order." It is our aim here to put Christ back into Christmas, to welcome the Christ Child in our souls, to enjoy the Godliness of having Christ's Mass at Christmas.

Merry Christmas to you! May Christ and His Mother bless you by their presence because of your goodness in giving to them your will and understanding during these Advent days.

Liturgical
Calendar by Year

Through Advent 2050

YEAR	2023 - B 2028 - A 2034 - C 2045 - B	2029 - B 2035 - A 2040 - C 2046 - C	2024 - C 2030 - C 2041 - A 2047 - A
1st Sun	Dec. 3	Dec. 2	Dec. 1
M	Dec. 4	Dec. 3	Dec. 2
T	Dec. 5	Dec. 4	Dec. 3
W	Dec. 6	Dec. 5	Dec. 4
Th	Dec. 7	Dec. 6	Dec. 5
F	**Immaculate Conception**	Dec. 7	Dec. 6
S	Dec. 9	**Immaculate Conception**	Dec. 7
2nd Sun	Dec. 10	Dec. 9	**Immaculate Conception**
M	Dec. 11	Dec. 10	Dec. 9
T	Dec. 12	Dec. 11	Dec. 10
W	Dec. 13	Dec. 12	Dec. 11
Th	Dec. 14	Dec. 13	Dec. 12
F	Dec. 15	Dec. 14	Dec. 13
S	Dec. 16	Dec. 15	Dec. 14
3rd Sun	17—O Wisdom	Dec. 16	Dec. 15
M	18—O Adonai	**17**—O Wisdom	Dec. 16
T	19—O Root of Jesse	18—O Adonai	**17**—O Wisdom
Ember W	20—O Key of David	19—O Root of Jesse	18—O Adonai
Th	21—O Rising Dawn	20—O Key of David	19—O Root of Jesse
Ember F	22—O King of the Nations	21—O Rising Dawn	20—O Key of David
Ember S	23—O Emmanuel	22—O King of the Nations	21—O Rising Dawn
4th Sun	**Christmas Eve**	23—O Emmanuel	22—O King of the Nations
M	**Christmas Day**	**Christmas Eve**	23—O Emmanuel
T	n/a	**Christmas Day**	**Christmas Eve**
W	n/a	n/a	**Christmas Day**
Th	n/a	n/a	n/a
F	n/a	n/a	n/a
S	n/a	n/a	n/a
Sun	n/a	n/a	n/a

2025 - A 2031 - A 2036 - B 2042 - B	2026 - B 2037 - C 2043 - C 2048 - B	2027 - C 2032 - B 2038 - A 2049 - C	2022 - A 2033 - C 2039 - B 2044 - A 2050 - A
Nov. 30	Nov. 29	Nov. 28	Nov. 27
Dec. 1	Nov. 30	Nov. 29	Nov. 28
Dec. 2	Dec. 1	Nov. 30	Nov. 29
Dec. 3	Dec. 2	Dec. 1	Nov. 30
Dec. 4	Dec. 3	Dec. 2	Dec. 1
Dec. 5	Dec. 4	Dec. 3	Dec. 2
Dec. 6	Dec. 5	Dec. 4	Dec. 3
Dec. 7	Dec. 6	Dec. 5	Dec. 4
Immaculate Conception	Dec. 7	Dec. 6	Dec. 5
Dec. 9	**Immaculate Conception**	Dec. 7	Dec. 6
Dec. 10	Dec. 9	**Immaculate Conception**	Dec. 7
Dec. 11	Dec. 10	Dec. 9	**Immaculate Conception**
Dec. 12	Dec. 11	Dec. 10	Dec. 9
Dec. 13	Dec. 12	Dec. 11	Dec. 10
Dec. 14	Dec. 13	Dec. 12	Dec. 11
Dec. 15	Dec. 14	Dec. 13	Dec. 12
Dec. 16	Dec. 15	Dec. 14	Dec. 13
17—O Wisdom	Dec. 16	Dec. 15	Dec. 14
18—O Adonai	**17**—O Wisdom	Dec. 16	Dec. 15
19—O Root of Jesse	18—O Adonai	**17**—O Wisdom	Dec. 16
20—O Key of David	19—O Root of Jesse	18—O Adonai	**17**—O Wisdom
21—O Rising Dawn	20—O Key of David	19—O Root of Jesse	18—O Adonai
22—O King of the Nations	21—O Rising Dawn	20—O Key of David	19—O Root of Jesse
23—O Emmanuel	22—O King of the Nations	21—O Rising Dawn	20—O Key of David
Christmas Eve	23—O Emmanuel	22—O King of the Nations	21—O Rising Dawn
Christmas Day	**Christmas Eve**	23—O Emmanuel	22—O King of the Nations
n/a	**Christmas Day**	**Christmas Eve**	23—O Emmanuel
n/a	n/a	**Christmas Day**	**Christmas Eve**
n/a	n/a	n/a	**Christmas Day**

Notes

- **A/B/C** — The letters indicated after the years refer to the corresponding cycle of readings from the *Lectionary for Mass* for the **Ordinary Form of the Roman Rite**. Thus, **Advent 2019** (and the rest of the 2020 liturgical year) used readings from Cycle A, while **Advent 2020** (and the rest of liturgical year 2021) used readings from Cycle B, and **Advent 2021** (and the rest of liturgical year 2022) used readings from Cycle C.

- **NB: The Extraordinary Form of the Roman Rite** does not have cycles, but has the same readings every year for its lectionary. As this work was written in 1953, all references to readings for the Mass and the Divine Office made in this work refer to the Roman liturgy prior to the Second Vatican Council.

- **4th Week of Advent** — The length for the season of Advent varies. The Fourth Sunday of Advent could be *as early as* Dec. 18, a full week before Christmas (as in 2016 and 2022), or not at all if it is on its latest date, December 24, as Christmas Eve is a more important liturgy (as in 2017 and 2023).

- **O Antiphons** — During the eight days before Christmas (December 17–24), the liturgy changes in an octave of preparation for Christmas day. The traditional "O Antiphons," which give various prophesied titles of the Messiah in the Old Testament, are used during the Evening Prayer of Liturgy of the Hours and in the Alleluia Verse before the Gospel reading at Mass. Additionally, special readings are used in this time during weekday Masses.

- **Ember Days** — "Ember days" are the days at the beginning of the seasons ordered by the Church as days of fast and abstinence. The purpose of their introduction, besides the general one intended by all prayer and fasting, was to thank God for the gifts of nature, to teach men to make use of them in moderation, and to assist the needy." They were definitely arranged and prescribed for the entire Church by Pope Gregory VII (1073–85) for the Wednesdays, Fridays, and Saturdays after St. Lucy's (December 13), after Ash Wednesday, after Pentecost, and after the Exaltation of the Cross (September 14).[2]

---

[2]   Francis Mershman, "Ember Days," *The Catholic Encyclopedia* Vol. 5 (New York: Robert Appleton Company, 1909).

SPIRITUAL STEPS
TO CHRISTMAS

First Week
of Advent

First Sunday of Advent:
Preparing for Christmas

"Jesus said to his disciples: 'There will be signs in the sun, the moon, and stars; and on the earth distress of nations, by reason of the confusion of the sound of the sea and of the waves, men withering away for fear and expectation of the things which shall come upon the world: for the powers of heaven shall be moved. And then they shall see the Son of man coming on a cloud with great power and majesty. But when these things begin to come to pass, look up, and lift up your heads: because your redemption is at hand.' And he spoke to them a similitude: 'See the fig-tree, and all the trees: when they now shoot forth their fruit, ye know that summer is nigh. So also, when the kingdom of God is at hand. Truly, I say to you, this generation will not pass away till all things be fulfilled. Heaven and earth shall pass away, but my words shall not pass away.'"[3] The Catholic Church is the most interesting institution in the world. Like her Founder, she is both human and divine. She is human because her members are of human origin; she is divine because Christ, the Head of these members, is divine. The Catholic Church is the greatest storyteller in the world. She is the greatest of all narrators because, being human, she is like a great nourishing mother, *Alma*[4] *Mater*, as she soothes her children with the happiest of tales in a most loving manner. She is the most profound and interesting storyteller, for she tells the story of God in His relations with men, the greatest story ever told: the story of God becoming man, the Incarnation.

Now, how does holy Mother Church tell this story and where does she get her facts? The Church tells the story by her liturgy, by her chant and, as it were, by painting word-pictures in the liturgy, thus arresting our attention by turning over the pages of the life of Christ for our spiritual growth.

The first Sunday of Advent marks the beginning of the storytelling by narrating the anticipation of Christ's coming and by highlighting the story in the word-picture of the day's liturgy. The liturgy of the Catholic Church is most impressive and contains a world of meaning if we will

---

[3]   Luke 21:25–33.

[4]   "Alma" is a Latin word which can be translated as "nourishing, kind, genial, or indulgent."

but look beneath the surface and meditate reflectively. Every movement of the priest and the people, every psalm, every prayer that is uttered has a meaning and contains a fund for spiritual enrichment that the witness is left to ponder in his heart and unlock the riches of wisdom.

It is our purpose in these thought pieces, in preparation for Christmas, to show the role that prayer and penance play in the life of each member of the Mystical Body of Christ to unlock these rich mysteries and truths. Thus, by a close following of the Gospels for the Sundays and by our thinking with the Church in a liturgical sense, we shall listen to the story related by our fostering, holy Mother Church concerning the greatest character of all history, Jesus Christ, true God and true man.

There is a pamphlet by Dom Gueranger[5] entitled, "Advent, Its Meaning and Purpose," which tells of the

---

[5] Dom Prosper Gueranger, OSB (1805–75) was a key figure in spreading the restoration of the Benedictine Order in the nineteenth century. Dom Gueranger was the founder and abbot of the Benedictine monastery at Solesmes, arguably one of the most powerful institutions in the recovering of beauty in the liturgy amid the liturgical decadence of post-Revolutionary and Napoleonic French Catholicism. His *magnum opus, The Liturgical Year*, is a fifteen volume work examining the Roman Liturgy, while under his leadership, his monastery compiled the authoritative book of chant, *Liber Usualis*, which the Roman Church adopted as the

preparation that should be made by Christian hearts before Christmas. In such a spirit of prayer during these Advent days, we come to the feet of our holy Mother; we listen to the most interesting of all storytellers and to the greatest story of them all. In spirit we go to a church in the City of Rome, St. Mary Major's, where we kneel before what holy tradition has presented to us as the Crib of Bethlehem.[6] On the first

---

liturgical book by which all chanted liturgies were sung, up until the promulgation of the *Novus Ordo Missae*.

[6] The Crib of Bethlehem is one of the oldest and longest revered relics of the Church. Saint Jerome had a great devotion to the Crib while it was in Bethlehem in the Patristic age, and the relic stayed there until the rise of Isalm in the seventh century jeopardized the relic's safety. Legend has it that Saint Jerome appeared to a monk three times, telling him to bring the relic to Rome. The holy relic was indeed taken to Rome where it has stayed since. The Crib is kept in Santa Maria Maggiore, also known as Saint Mary's Major, Our Lady of the Snow, and Our Lady of the Crib, due to a few pieces of wood being kept on the altar. On Christmas night, the rest of the relics in their majestic reliquaries are brought in a solemn procession to the main altar of the church and stay there for three days for public venearation. In 2019, a small part of the Crib was sent to Bethlehem under the protection of the Custodia Terrae Sanctae at Saint Catherine's Church, which is adjacent to the Church of the Nativity. See *Sacred Heart Review*, Volume 3, Number 2, December 7, 1889; See also "Vatican returns Jesus 'crib fragment' to Bethlehem," *DW*, accessed June 2, 2022, http://dw.com/en/vatican-returns-jesus-crib-fragment-to-bethehem/a-51463805.

Sunday of Advent all Christians in the spirit of the liturgy of the Mass make their way to this station. It is for this reason we find the prayers of the Mass centering around the birth of Christ and the Virgin Mother and the crib.

The story of the long awaiting for the coming of Christ is told in the words of Isaiah the prophet, who of all the prophets Sacred Scripture speaks most directly and explicitly of the Messiah. For each day of Advent, Holy Mother Church has her priests and religious pray something from the writings of this great prophet in their recitation of the Divine Office.

In this prophecy Isaiah speaks of the Lord, who exalted His children only to have them despise Him; he speaks of Israel, "who hath not known the Lord and His people, who hath not understood." And he continues: "They have forsaken the Lord, they have blasphemed the Holy One of Israel; they have gone backwards."[7]

The words of the Prophet should make a deep impression on our hearts at the beginning of the holy season of Advent. Who of us can hear without trembling this voice of the Lord, who is despised and unknown even at the very time when He is to come and visit His people? "If today you hear His voice, harden not your hearts."[8]

---

[7] Isaiah 1:3–4.

[8] Psalm 94:8.

The story is being retold. The Church, in accents of solemnity, in colors of penitential purple vestments, in notes of solemn music is repeating for us the burden of her message. Christ is coming to save the world, which, as Isaias says, is sickened—"the whole head is sick and the whole heart is sad."[9] Christ is coming to judge the world, for "the powers of heaven shall be moved, and then they shall see the Son of man coming on a cloud with great power and majesty. When these things begin to come to pass, look up, and lift up your heads, because your redemption is at hand."[10]

Members of Christ's Mystical Body, hearken to the words of "the greatest story ever told" as recounted by the greatest mother of them all. The story is Christ's coming, or Advent. The mother is the Church. Now is the hour for us to rise from sleep, to save the world from chaos, to rescue souls from materialism, and to save them for the all-powerful dignity of incorporation in Christ's Mystical Body. We shall do this by beginning to reform ourselves, by spending Advent prayerfully, by "casting off the works of darkness . . . and putting on the Lord Jesus Christ."[11]

---

[9] Isaiah 1:5.
[10] Luke 21:26–28.
[11] Romans 13:12, 14.

Prayer

Blessed Savior of men, You prepared us, Your servants, for long years by prophecies and symbols to foretell of the Coming of the Anointed One, the Messiah, who would redeem the world and reopen for us the gates of Paradise.

This Advent we pray and beseech You to accept our humble offering of preparation of our bodies and souls. May each day be for us a step, each step a prayer, each prayer a pilgrimage toward Bethlehem with Jesus and Mary and Joseph. Help us to pray fervently, to walk valiantly, and to persevere to the end, You who live and reign with the Father in the unity of the Holy Spirit, God, forever and ever. Amen.

Monday of the First Week of Advent: Christmas Is the Feast of the Home

G. K. Chesterton has noted that Christmas is a divine paradox. Christmas is the Feast of the Homeless One who had to find shelter in a cave and to be warmed by the breath of oxen, yet the same feast is celebrated in every home. For this reason it is good for us in this holy season of Advent to reflect on the importance of the home and Christian civilization.

One of the most historic shrines of France, attended annually by thousands of visitors, is Malmaison, the home of Napoleon and Josephine. It was here that Napoleon came after his brilliant military victories. Each room is arranged exactly in the same manner as when this great military leader occupied it. There is the very chair in which sat this monarch of world empire, there is the desk at which he wrote, and there the pen with which he mapped out his great victories.

As the visitor passes through these rooms exuding a martial atmosphere, he comes into the suite occupied by Josephine. There is a marked contrast. No martial note here. Only the little incidentals that minister to the needs of womankind and echo forth the dominant note of her heart are present. True, here in this room is a beautiful harp, a symbol of domestic peace and homely concord. Upon further inspection, however, we note that its strings are broken. It stands there mute and silent as an ironic reminder that discordant notes of domestic strife once filled this chamber. To every informed visitor it is a symbol and a reminder that the great Napoleon who conquered Europe failed in the altogether crucial building of the most important empire of all—the empire of his own home. Indeed, the inspired writer has written the epitaph for this story when he said: "Greater is he who governs himself than he who rules cities."[12]

With the authority as the Vicar of Christ coupled with the kindly voice of a shepherd caring for his sheep, Pope Pius XI's papal encyclical *Casti Connubii* reminds all peoples that the home is the foundation of human society.[13] He who undermines the home, the Father of Christendom points out, blasts at the solid bedrock upon which not only society but all stable government alike is built. No expedient yet devised by the sociologist or political scientist constitutes so mighty a bulwark for the protection of human society and orderly government as the teaching of Christ's Church concerning the sanctity of marriage, the indissolubility of its bond, and the permanence of the Christian home.

---

[12] Proverbs 16:32.

[13] "How great is the dignity of chaste wedlock, Venerable Brethren, may be judged best from this that Christ Our Lord, Son of the Eternal Father, having assumed the nature of fallen man, not only, with His loving desire of compassing the redemption of our race, ordained it in an especial manner as the principle and foundation of domestic society and therefore of all human intercourse, but also raised it to the rank of a truly and great sacrament of the New Law, restored it to the original purity of its divine institution, and accordingly entrusted all its discipline and care to His spouse the Church." Pope Pius XI, *Casti Connubii* (December 31, 1930), no. 1.

The mother is the "heart," the father is the "head" of the home. It is the plan of an all-wise and provident God that a child be reared in a home where principles of proper thought and action are instilled by a loving mother and a kindly ruling father. After years of study and research, experts in child psychology now assure us that impressions received during early childhood undoubtedly set up mental patterns and modes of conduct, in the light of which all the experiences of later life are interpreted and evaluated. Indeed, this is merely an affirmation of a truth spoken thousands of years ago by the inspired writer of the Book of Proverbs, wherein we read: "Train up a child in the way he should go, and when he is old he will not depart from it."[14]

The home dominated by the mother and father occupies the all-important position in life, for the most important things are their primary concerns. A mother need not be learned as measured by worldly standards; she need only have a knowledge of God and a loving, kindly, living fear of the Lord in order successfully to train her child. A father need not know the ways and means of ruling an empire! Indeed, if he did, he, like the great Napoleon, might neglect the empire of his home. A father need only

---

[14] Proverbs 22:6.

have an understanding of the words, "the fear of the Lord is the beginning of wisdom,"[15] and live out and instruct his children in this wisdom. Such a father placed in rule over a child, with his loving spouse at his side, is indeed the builder of nations and is beloved of God!

Our Holy Father Pope Pius XII reminds us in his encyclical letter on "Christian Education"[16] that the home precedes both the Church and the State in the matter of education.[17] For, since the mother is the first and most effective teacher of the child, the home becomes the first and most important school. No lay teacher, sister, or priest can be an adequate substitute for the mother as a teacher.

---

[15] Proverbs 9:10.

[16] Pope Pius XII, *Divini Illistrius Magistri* (December 29, 1931).

[17] "The Angelic Doctor with his wonted clearness of thought and precision of style, says: 'The father according to the flesh has in a particular way a share in that principle which in a manner universal is found in God. . . . The father is the principle of generation, of education and discipline and of everything that bears upon the perfecting of human life.' (S.T., 2-2, Q. 102, a. 1) The family therefore holds directly from the Creator the mission and hence the right to educate the offspring, a right inalienable because inseparably joined to the strict obligation, a right anterior to any right whatever of civil society and of the State, and therefore inviolable on the part of any power on earth." Pope Pius XII, *Divini Illistrius Magistri*, nos. 31, 32).

These agencies are only meant to be complementary and supplementary to the training given the child in the home.

The Church for our edification and inspiration points to the model home of Nazareth, where Jesus dwelt in obedience to Mary and Joseph. Thus did our divine Lord set up an example for youth everywhere, for Scripture tells us, "He was subject to them."[18]

Great has been the example of good homes through the ages! Look to the saintly influences of St. Monica in praying for her son, Augustine. Look to the example of the queenly mother Blanche and her influence over her son, St. Louis of France. Look about the world today and wherever you see priests and sisters you will know the influence of the home that is good. Look into your own heart today! Remember the joys of your happy home life! Is it any wonder that a ballad comes down through the years, sung by a thousand voices, a thousand times over, "Home, Sweet Home"?

Somewhere in heaven today there is a mother reaping the reward of a Christian home she founded upon earth. To such noble women we pledge our loyalty to preserve these ideals for America, under God, and in filial devotion and prayer, we say:

---

[18] Luke 2:51.

Mother, upon me gaze tonight
    From thy beautiful home above;

And tell me are the stars as bright
    As the beacon of thy love?

Mother, does sometimes upon thy knee
    While the angels stand and stare,

The Christ-Child sit and tell thee of me,
    And finger thy silvery hair?

Mother, when life's short years are run,
    And the Gleaner beckons to me,

Oh, pray the God in that Little One
    To bring me home to thee.

Tuesday of the First Week of Advent: God's Star

A soldier's best prayer is always one motivated by hope, and not by fear. Strange, too—or is it strange?—that the greatest act of love, an act of perfect contrition, is one motivated not by fear of punishment, but by deep and abiding love for God! The expression "there are no atheists in foxholes" has grown old with World War II, but its meaning is read in a thousand different dispatches from the battlefront of life itself. The soldier who goes bravely to his death is not alone! He is mindful of Another who carried a cross to Calvary and who won the only victory that matters. In this our day we must all be soldiers of Christ, for we are such by the sacrament of Confirmation.

It is told of Sir Harry Lauder[19] that while he was in Melbourne, Australia, and had just sustained the loss of his only son, who had fallen at the front, he related the following beautiful incident: "A man came to my dressing room in a New York theater and told of an experience that had recently befallen him. In American towns, any household that had given a son to the war was entitled to place a star on the windowpane. Well, a few nights

---

19   Sir Harry Lauder (1870–1950) was a Scottish singer and comedian, and he was quite popular in the United States.

before he came to see me, this man was walking down a street in New York accompanied by his wee little boy. The lad became very interested in the lighted windows of the houses and clapped his hands when he saw a star. As they passed house after house he would say, 'Oh, look, Daddy, there's another house that has given a son to the war. And there's another. There's one with two stars. And look, there's a house with no star at all.' At last they came to a break in the houses. Through the gap could be seen the evening star shining brightly in the sky. The little fellow caught his breath. 'Oh, look, Daddy,' he cried, 'God must have given His Son, for He has a star in His window!'" God's star in heaven's window tells of Christmas when God gave His Son to the world. This is the story of God's love in the Incarnation.

The soldier who prays before he goes into battle is the man who is conscious of the fact that he goes not alone. He is acutely aware that God is with him and that the Son of God went into the darkness of Calvary when man warred upon divinity in the terrible crucifixion that led to the victory of Easter. God foresaw His death even as He planned His birth at Bethlehem. For Bethlehem and Calvary are cycles. In His birth and in His death is our life and our redemption.

"Today every Christian is a soldier—soldier of Christ," said the convert Charles Péguy one time. "The least among us is a soldier. Our fathers, like a flood of people, like a flood of armies, invaded the infidel continents. Nowadays, on the contrary, it is a flood of infidelity that holds the seas, the high seas, and continuously assails us from all sides. All our houses are fortresses, in danger of the mighty sea. The holy war is everywhere. It is ever being waged. All of us stand on the breach today. We are stationed at the frontier. The frontier is everywhere. . . ."[20] Indeed, each and every Christian is called to live this out in his daily life, ever remembering the words of St. Paul: "For if we have been planted together in the likeness of his death, we shall be also in the likeness of his resurrection."[21]

Prayer

Blessed Savior, I know so well the meaning of grace and yet I permit its lesson to escape me. I know full well that grace is best received by a heart humble and contrite and ready to welcome its God. I know, too, that such readiness requires vigilance and prayer—"watch and pray" are the words of Advent as well as Lent, for Bethlehem and Calvary and Easter are all one great event—they are but steppingstones

---

[20] *Basic Verities* (New York: Pantheon Books, Inc., 1943).

[21] Romans 6:5.

to heaven. Teach me to prepare this Advent for an increase of grace and a fuller understanding of the Redemption and Incarnation. You who live and reign with the Father in the unity of the Holy Spirit, God, forever and ever. Amen.

Wednesday of the First Week of Advent: The Meaning of Advent

Our day begs for more emphasis upon the teaching of the Church and the meaning of Advent. There is need for more prayer and penance. There is need for a greater faith. There is need for holiness. Advent is the season of preparation when by prayer and mortification we ensure our hearts are being better disposed for the coming of Christ on the holy and blessed day of Christmas. The only way to gauge the future is to plan the present well. A good preparation today is the best guarantee of a work to be accomplished well tomorrow. Holy Mother Church knows that the only way to have security and peace of a spiritual nature tomorrow is to build well during the season of Advent, which for you and me, dear reader, is today.

Jesus Christ is the same today, yesterday, and forever. His Church, like any healthy organism, meets the needs of the present. She has thrown off and survived the heresies of the past, and she gives assurance of living in the future, both in this world and the one to come.

The Church knows something of the world of yesterday, for she has cherished its goodness, preserved its culture, and transmitted the past's riches to today. She has the right to speak of the world of tomorrow, for in her Advent blessings and in her divine assurance she knows what is ultimately to come: "the gates of Hell shall not prevail against her." She has plans for the present. It is the blueprint and charter of the word of God and the eternal plan of Christ which can never grow old or out of date, for it is impossible for the eternal truths of God to change with the passing of time. Every time and age submits to the authority of the Church, the Bride of Christ, and we, her children, are no different. But it is not a harsh yoke under which we place ourselves, but a loving one. If we are to gain that security and peace of a spiritual nature that awaits us on Christmas day, then we must put ourselves with full confidence and trust under the caring tutelage of Holy Mother Church. This time of placing ourselves under the guardianship of another is not limited to the Church, but also applies to Our Lady and the saints.

There is a story told of a strong virile soldier most grievously wounded in World War I. He was dying. When taken to a hospital it was discovered that a bullet lay lodged close to his heart. To touch it would have meant almost certain death. Three times the surgeon began his work, then desisted and laid down the scalpel. After a few days the bullet moved, in a mysterious manner, to another position. The operation was performed and the patient lived. The soldier asked the doctor why he had three times prepared to operate, and yet three times hesitated. The surgeon answered and said, "Because I saw a young girl before me who caught hold of my hand." "A young girl?" asked the soldier. "Would you recognize her from a photograph?" A picture of St. Thérèse, the Little Flower of Jesus, was shown the doctor. "Was it she?" "Yes," replied the doctor, "it was certainly she!" Ever since that day fresh roses are placed daily in that soldier's drawing room in the city of Paris in memory of this heavenly intervention in his behalf as an example of their devotion and faith to the great saints of Lisieux.

The Church during the holy season of Advent emphasizes for all Catholics the great need for prayer and faith if we are to succeed in establishing our close identity with Christ, the Head of the Mystical Body. Our Alma Mater, our great nourishing Mother the Church, asks us to hearken to the words of the greatest story ever told, the story of Christ's coming, the story of Bethlehem. It can best be learned by prayer and meditation and hearkening to your Mother's voice. She will lead you along the way she knows so well and which terminates at the feet of God, wrapped in swaddling clothes and laid in a manger.

Prayer

Dear Mother of Christ, we love you and pledge our devotion to you. As children upon our mother's knee, we recall the blessings of childhood, the lullabies our loveliest of mothers used to sing. When the years turned her lovely locks to gray, we cherished her the more, till God called her. You, O Mary, are our Mother in heaven and on earth. We need this Christmastide and Advent season to hear a heavenly lullaby. Sing to us, O Mary, the songs of heaven that earth may not hold us in its grip. We were made for God, and restless children are we, till we return through you to Him, Who lives and reigns with the Father in the unity of the Holy Spirit, God, forever and ever. Amen.

Thursday of the First Week of Advent: Happy New Year

The world is old, but the Church—ever ancient and ever new—is young.

A mortal does not look forward to old age with joy or jubilation. He may look forward to a day of accomplishment when he will be able to say, "I have finished," or to some long-cherished hope fulfilled, but no one of us can honestly say we celebrate our birthday anniversary with joy and exultation because we are older by a year. What, then, does age give us to occasion joy? Rather, does it not bring us closer to the portal of death? Does it not separate us each year further from the period of our youth? True, all too true—but age brings us also closer to maturity of mind and advances us in the realm of the spirit, closer to God. Our bodies grow old, but our intellect and will, faculties of the soul, become keener and more disciplined, thanks to the great faith that we have inherited and for which our Lord and Savior Jesus Christ suffered and died, so that we might be children of God and heirs of heaven.

Thus, Advent is the dawn of a liturgically new year. We grow older in age, but, please God, closer to our ambition and goal: a good life, a greater devotion to duty and to our neighbor, and an assurance of eternal life.

The world grows old, but the Church is ever young. Hence it is that as our bodies grow old and feeble, our souls grow not feeble in hope but advance in wisdom and grace before God and men. While our bodies slow down with the passage of time, our spiritual lives are spurred on with the promise of immortality on the part of One who is faithful to His promises. Our intellects grow closer to becoming images of the divine intellect by increasing in knowledge and thus ability to love God more. Our wills, disciplined by prayer which makes them one with the divine will and by sacrifice which curbs our lower nature, makes us more like unto Christ who came that we might have life in abundance.

Every new ecclesiastical year of the Advent season has meaning for the Catholic heart. The new reminds us to reflect upon the old, not for the sake of regrets, but for the purpose of greater progress for the future. Each penitential season of Advent renews hope in the Christian heart and a promise that the Redeemer is near.

The new year can be a year of hope and Christian living, or it can be one in which deeds are prompted not by the higher, moral law, but by the inclinations of fallen man. Our task and resolution for Advent is to prepare for the possibilities ahead, for a better Christian life. Every man and woman, born of Adam, is heir to all the faults of the human race. "The corruption of the best is the worst," the old adage says. The saints' accomplishment of reaching the heights is chiefly attributable to the fact that they were conscious of their human frailty and relied upon the strength of God's grace.

Prayer and the Christian life of sacrifice modeled after Christ and Mary will be the tool with which we may each day of the new year work away until we have formed in our souls the image and likeness of a real Catholic. We have ideals. We have memories. We have had a good mother, a kindly father, noble brothers and sisters. We have gone ahead with the years, nourished by the life of the Church's sacraments. The world may have tarnished our hopes, our aspirations, but it cannot destroy our faith! We move on with the Church and with the assurance that age cannot destroy but can only give fulfillment to our life with God.

Prayer

Blessed Savior of men, help us to count our years in terms of acts of service for You and for our fellow man, worthy of the reward of eternal life. Were we a thousand times thankful, still would we be unworthy servants. Enlighten our minds, strengthen our wills, and give us an ever-growing desire to reach our true celestial fatherland. With Your grace, we resolve to watch and pray the new year that peace and justice may return to mankind, and we grow in holiness as living models of your Sacred Heart. You who live and reign with the Father in the unity of the Holy Spirit, God, forever and ever. Amen.

First Friday of Advent:
Going Home

The poet, John Howard Payne,[22] has memorialized for all times the ballad, "Home, Sweet Home," of which the opening lines, so familiar to most of us, are:

> Mid pleasures and palaces though we
> may roam,
>
> Be it ever so humble, there's no place
> like home.

Sometime ago there was shown in the newsreel theaters, under the sponsorship of "This Is America," a film dealing with marriage and the home entitled, "Courtship and the Courthouse," in which there was dramatically portrayed the great danger that faces America today when almost one out of every four marriages ends in divorce.[23]

---

[22]   John Howard Payne (1791–1852) was an American poet, actor, playwright, and author.

[23]   The percentage as of 2021 from the United States' Center for Disease Control is that 41 percent of all first marriages end in divorce in the United States, while 50 percent of all marriages end in divorce. "FASTSTATS - Marriage and Divorce," Centers for Disease Control and Prevention, March 25, 2022. https://www.cdc.gov/nchs/fastats/marriage-divorce.htm.

From the watchtower of the eternal city, Pope Pius XII, surveying with a master's eye the subversive forces of anti-Christ and atheism, has sounded a warning to the world on the dangers that strike at the very foundations of human society. He cautions us to beware of those who would destroy the sanctity of the home.

In the liturgy of the Church, we read of the obedience of Christ to His Blessed Mother and to St. Joseph.[24] St. Paul tells us of the virtues that go to make up a good home when he says:

> "Be ye all, therefore, as the elect of God, holy and beloved, the soul of mercy, benignity, humility, modesty, patience. Bearing with one another and forgiving one another, if any have a complaint against another even as the Lord hath forgiven you, so do you also. . . . Wives, be subject to your husbands as it behooveth in the Lord. Husbands, love your wives and be not bitter towards them. Children, obey your parents in all things; for this is well pleasing to the Lord. . . . Whatsoever you do, do it from the heart, as to the Lord, and not

---

[24] Luke 2:51.

to men. Knowing that you shall receive
of the Lord the reward of inheritance.
Serve ye the Lord Christ."[25]

The universe is God's home, and if men would only look up to God they would be at home even in their adversities. The United Nations is trying to build a home for the universality of mankind, but there can be no universality and there can be no home without God. Thus the Psalmist explains, "O Lord our God, how admirable is thy name in the whole earth! . . . What is man that thou art mindful of him? or the son of man that thou visitest him? Thou hast made him a little less than the angels, thou hast crowned him with glory and honour, and hast set him over the works of thy hands. . . . O Lord our Lord, how admirable is thy name in all the earth."[26]

The world is God's home and God is at home in the world. There is nothing that man can do to expel God from the universe. Foolishly—for it is only the fool who would so act—do men try to expel God from the world He has made.

God is at home in the soul of man as often as man sets his will in accord with the will of God. God is present in the houses of both rich and poor as often as a man and wife

---

[25] Col. 3:12–24.
[26] Psalm 8:1–10.

live in accordance with the moral laws of the Creator. Man can make houses, but only God can make a home.

Advent tells us of our going home to God. Christmas means God with us.

Christmas reminds us of the great beneficence of God. Of Him it was said, "unto His own He came and His own received Him not."[27] Into our own hearts this Sacred Heart would come this Christmas, if we would but open them to receive Him. The heart of a God beat in the breast of a Child at Bethlehem, and that same heart was pierced on Calvary—the very heart of God.

The Sacred Heart of God bleeds for us anew every time a sin is committed, as St. Paul tells us that sin crucifies Christ all over again, and to St. Margaret Mary Alacoque Christ confided that the world should make reparation to this Heart that loves us so much. Christ asks good souls to repair the damage of sin.

If a mother can give of the substance of her body to feed her child—if a father can, under God, generate new life and sustain it by his toil, sweat, and very blood—why cannot the members of the Church which is Christ's Mystical Body give prayers and sacrifices to make amends to the Heart of Christ for their fellow men who sin?

---

[27] John 1:11.

Soldiers on battlefields give their blood that we may live in freedom. The least a good soldier of Christ might do is bleed a little in a spiritual way by penance as an offering of reparation to the Sacred Heart of Christ.

Home is where the heart is, and our hearts ought to be at home only with God. This is the meaning of First Friday reparation.

The Church canonized Margaret Mary, who is known to us by the Twelve Promises made by our Lord to her. The Church encourages the faithful to make a Communion of Reparation on each First Friday because of the revelations and to make the Nine First Fridays because of the wonderful Twelfth Promise: "I promise thee in the excessive mercy of my Heart that my all-powerful love will grant to all those who communicate on the First Friday in nine consecutive months the grace of final penitence; they shall not die in my disgrace nor without receiving their Sacraments. My divine Heart shall be their safe refuge in this last moment."

Into our homes He will come, if we will but make them truly Christian, for Christmas is the feast day of the home. If we will make of our hearts a tabernacle, He will come to dwell in them through His grace. If we will but make our homes truly Christian, He will come to sanctify our homes and our nation.

Prayer

O Lady of Heaven, Mary, you were homeless at Bethlehem and had to travel afar to escape the wrath of a wicked King. Joseph, your faithful spouse, never faltered, but worked humbly and incessantly to make a home for you and Jesus. Heaven is our home and we are always truant children unless we direct our every step toward heaven and you. Mary, intercede with God for grace on our behalf that we may never wander from the path that leads to our heavenly home. We ask this through Our Lord Jesus Christ, your son, who lives and reigns with the Father in the unity of the Holy Spirit, God, forever and ever. Amen.

First Saturday of Advent: Promise of Peace

The Peace of Christ is the most dear thing anyone can ask for in this world, and this same peace extended to the world has been the dream of kings and peasants since time immemorial. Our Lady of Fatima, appearing to three little shepherd children, Jacinta, aged seven, Francisco, aged nine, and Lucia, aged ten, on a plateau outside the village Cova da Iria (in Fatima, a Portuguese town about sixty miles north of Lisbon), made some promises regarding the peace of the world that are particularly pertinent at this time, and prophesied to bring about the peace of Christ to our souls this Christmas, and to prepare our souls to welcome her Son this new liturgical year.

With a smile of maternal tenderness, yet somewhat sad, she beckoned gently to the children to approach, saying: "Have no fear, I will do you no harm. I come from heaven. I want you children to come here on the thirteenth of each month, until October. Then I will tell you who I am."

On July 13, 1917, after the children had seen the apparition of Our Lady again, as promised, they were permitted to behold the fires of hell, after which the following prophecy was delivered:

"You have seen the inferno where the souls of sinners end. To save souls our Lord desires that devotion to my Immaculate Heart be established in the world.

"If what I tell you is done, many souls will be saved and there will be peace. The war will end; but if they do not cease to offend the Lord, not much time will elapse, and precisely during the next Pontificate, another and more terrible war will commence. When a night illumination by an unknown light is seen, know that is the signal that God gives you that the castigation of the world for its many transgressions is at hand, through war, famine, and persecution of the Church and the Holy Father. To prevent this, I ask the consecration of the world to my Immaculate Heart, and Communion in reparation on the first Saturday of each month."

August 13 found more than 15,000 people at the Cova da Iria. More than 30,000 people gathered there on September 13; and again on October 13, despite incessant rain, an enormous crowd of more than 70,000 assembled from all corners of Portugal and far distant places in Europe.

On this latter occasion the beautiful Lady appeared to the children for the last time, more radiant than ever before. "Her face was brighter than the sun," said Francisco, who was dazzled, but yet unable to withdraw his gaze. To the question, "Who are you and what do you wish?" placed by Lucia, the answer came:

"I am the Lady of the Rosary and I have come to warn the faithful to amend their lives and ask pardon for their sins. They must not continue to offend our Lord, already so deeply offended. They must say the Rosary."

Our Blessed Mother also declared that she wished a Church built at the Cova da Iria in honor of Our Lady of the Rosary, and that if the people amended their lives the war would soon end.

The apparitions of Our Lady have received the seal of approval of the Church as worthy of our belief, and the devotion was authorized under the title of Our Lady of the Rosary. Millions of pilgrims have visited Fatima; and in a five-year period 215 miraculous cures were claimed. Fatima is fast becoming a world center of Mary's wonders and intercession.

Pope Pius XII asked all to pray to Our Lady of Fatima. He has dedicated the world to her Immaculate Heart. During Advent, and, indeed, every first Saturday of the month pray for peace—peace for the world, peace for our country, peace for our families, and peace for our own souls.

Prayer

Queen of the Most Holy Rosary, Refuge of the human race, Victress in all God's battles, we humbly prostrate ourselves before your throne, confident that we shall receive mercy, grace, and bountiful assistance and protection in the present calamity, not through our own inadequate merits, but solely through the great goodness of your maternal heart. We ask this through Our Lord Jesus Christ, your son, who lives and reigns with the Father in the unity of the Holy Spirit, God, forever and ever. Amen.

SECOND
WEEK OF ADVENT

Second Sunday of Advent:
Prayer Means Progress

"When John had heard in prison the words of Christ, sending two of his disciples he said to him: Art thou he that is to come, or look we for another? And Jesus answering said to them: Go and relate to John what you have heard and seen. The blind see, the lame walk, the lepers are cleansed, the deaf hear, the dead rise again, the poor have the gospel preached to them; and blessed is he that shall not be scandalized in me. And when they went their way, Jesus began to say to the multitudes concerning John: What went ye out into the desert to see? A reed shaken with the wind? But what went ye out to see? A man clothed in soft garments? Behold, they that are clothed in soft garments, are in the houses of kings. But what went ye out to see? A prophet? Yea, I tell you, and more than a prophet. For this is he of whom it is written: Behold, I send my angel before thy face, who shall prepare thy way before thee."[28]

We have said that the Church, in her Advent story, tells us the most beautiful of all the stories of earth, the story of God becoming man. Today, and every Advent day, she continues the tale. Just as a great artist uses many colors to bring out the beauty of his detail—and yet there is always one dominant color—and just as a tapestry weaver uses many colored threads to beautify the design—and yet there always remains a prominent hue in his texture—so the greatest mother of them all, holy Mother Church, paints for us today, by her liturgy of Advent, the picture of Christ's coming, and the dominant thread in the great detail of this tapestry of beauty which she is weaving is that of courage. The Divine Office of the Church is filled with the notes of joy, hope, and courage with which the soul awaiting Christ should be animated.

Holy Mother Church says today to every Catholic heart: "Come with me." As loyal subjects, as children, we follow and in spirit we pass over the waters to a church in the City of Jerusalem, the Basilica of the Holy Cross. In the language of Sacred Scripture, Jerusalem is the image of the soul dedicated to God. From the cross we are to take

---

[28] Matthew 11:2–10.

courage and hope. Of old the cross was an instrument of crucifixion. It was an object of horror and derision, but today, by virtue of the grace of God, the cross is an object of veneration. From the cross comes courage. From the cross comes hope. From the cross comes our holy religion. St. Thomas à Kempis says, "In the cross is joy of spirit, in the cross is freedom from our enemies. Take up your cross and follow Jesus and you shall enter into eternal life." Holy Mother Church bids us to heed the cross, and so we shall look to that in our preparation for Christmas.

Guided by her divine Spouse, our infallible teacher and guide now conducts us gently into the liturgy of the Mass, and, in the Epistle and Gospel, we hear again the dominant note of courage inspired by a strong faith, a lively hope, and an ardent charity.

In the Epistle,[29] St. Paul, the great Apostle to the Gentiles, says: "Brethren, whatsoever things were written, were written for our learning; that through patience and the comfort of the Scriptures we might have hope." Again the great Apostle exhorts us to rejoice. In the day's Gospel,[30] we are exhorted to have faith in Jesus, for "the blind see, the lame walk, the lepers are cleansed, the deaf hear, the dead rise again, and the poor have the Gospel preached

---

[29] Romans 15:4–13.
[30] Matthew 11:2–10.

to them." Here is the groundwork of our courage, a deep faith in Jesus Christ.

Finally, the third of the three virtues must be manifest in our courage: charity. This greatest of the virtues makes us most like unto God, who is love,[31] just as the lack of it makes us most like unto the devil, who hates so fiercely! The members of Christ's Mystical Body must be motivated by love if their courage is to have deep-rooted effects. The members who compose the anti-Christ's body have no place in their meetings for charity. Their Gospel is one of hatred. Red truly is the color of a heart inflamed, red is the color of martyrs, and red is the color of the Holy Spirit, the Spirit of love and charity. We must revolutionize not bodies in rebellions of hate, but souls in rebellion against sin. Members of Christ's Mystical Body must be motivated by love for God. This battle of courage and love must be waged under *our* banner of red, which symbolizes the martyrs' blood and the Holy Spirit, the Spirit of love.

Like Christian warriors of old, fully armored in faith, hope, and charity, which constitute the armor of God, by Advent prayer and penance we will find our courage renewed! Despite the hardships of life and the perversities

---

[31] I John 4:16.

of men, we "will take up arms against a sea of troubles and by opposing end them,"[32] for God is on our side.

Let us not think that this battle can be won except with the grace of God.[33] Holy Mother Church takes us in the spirit of the liturgy to Jerusalem, the city typifying the faithful soul. The Church in accents of liturgical chant and in colors of penitential purple shows us the holy cross and its reliquary, the Basilica at Jerusalem, in order to stir up our courage motivated by faith, hope, and charity. The Church gives us a model in today's Gospel, St. John the Baptist, who was not a reed shaken by the wind, nor a man clothed in soft garments, but rather a prophet, of whom it was written, "I send my angel before thy face, who shall prepare thy way before thee."

Though wounded, diseased, and maimed by sin, we can win this battle—but only with Christ! Are we blind? Then let us come to Him who is the Light of the world. Are we lame? He will cure us so that we can walk! Do we suffer from the leprosy of sin? He will cleanse us! Are we deaf to the dangers of perversion corrupting even the very

---

[32] *Hamlet*, Act III, Scene I, ll. 67-68. (The third and fourth lines from the famous soliloquy of Hamlet, "To be or not to be.")

[33] John 15:5—" I am the vine, you are the branches: He that stays in me, and I in him, the same brings forth much fruit: for *without me you can do nothing*."

salt of the earth? He will cause us to listen to the sweet inspiration of God's grace in our souls! Are we dead in sin? He will make us live the life of grace, the life of God. Are we poor? He will preach to us the Kingdom of Heaven, where "neither rust nor moth doth consume, nor thieves break through to steal."[34]

Come, Lord Jesus, we pray, come into our souls, renew our courage with deep sentiments of faith, hope, and charity. The world needs Your Advent! My soul needs Your Advent! The world, as Isaias has said, is sickened and the whole body is sad. Yet, we have ardent hope, for, like the voice of the captain on the bridge in a stormy peril at sea, we can hear above the din and noise of the turbulent waves the voice of our Master, "Lo, I am with you all days even unto the consummation of the world."[35]

Prayer

Dear Jesus, teach me to forgive even my enemies that I may be forgiven. Show me the true motive of love which binds up the wounds and refuses to count the cost. Calvary is our great lesson; help me to reflect upon it every day of my life. Bethlehem and Calvary are cycles—returning over and over again and teaching me of God's love and

---

[34] Matthew 6:20.
[35] Matthew 28:20.

forgiveness. The Babe at Bethlehem and the God-Man on the cross both—the one and same divinity—extend arms of love and mercy. Grant me the grace to embrace and comply with the graces of each that You offer to me daily. You who live and reign with the Father in the unity of the Holy Spirit, God, forever and ever. Amen.

Monday of the Second Week of Advent: Unrequited Love

One of the great tragedies of life is finding one, upon whom so much love and kindness has been bestowed, totally unconscious of the gifts that have been so abundantly bestowed upon him. Sometimes it happens that a wife is untrue to a husband. She may even be the mother of children, in which case we should expect to find an increase of that love which is so characteristic of womankind, and yet, somehow, the true stream of human affection has become poisoned and love is unrequited. Passion sometimes takes the place of true love, and where affection should abound hatred and disappointment take its place.

The dictum *corruptio optimi pessima*—"The corruption of the best is the worst" typifies what we mean. The greatest harm is often done *not* by those who have no knowledge of the faith, but by those who once were infused with divine goodness and love and then permitted their illumined minds and inspired wills to become perverted and corrupted.

When those who once loved each other in marriage and were two in one flesh decide to separate, the human race loses a partnership and receives a blow that strikes at the very cornerstone of the social structure. When husband and wife decide that what once was a beautiful romance and an ardent love has now ceased to hold any attraction, not only do they personally suffer a loss, but through them and the solidarity of the human race all mankind suffers.

Unrequited love is the tragedy of our day. Passion is mistaken for affection and love is confused with lust and sin as though love consisted only of sensual satisfaction and concupiscence. The Church, replete with the wisdom of the ages, stands as the beacon of light in the tempest that surrounds the shipwrecked folly of our age. The Church proclaims the blessedness of marital union, and while she is thoroughly conscious of the powerful instincts found in every man and woman and entrusted by almighty God for the propagation of the race and for the allaying of concupiscence, wise Mother that she is, she emphasizes the tender affections of the human heart that can be nurtured only on the finer things of the spirit.

Those who have experienced the conflicts that arise between spouses and who have spent long hours in listening to marital difficulties and in giving advice, tell us that most of the pain that is caused and most of the rifts that occur are occasioned by little things, such as the tone of voice, attitudes, the irate response, the lack of attention, and the many little irritants of daily living.

It is a common fault of human nature, and one of which many of us are frequently guilty, that we fail properly to appreciate the little courtesies that make life easier and our neighbor's lot a trifle less difficult.

Unrequited love is one of the tragedies of America's divorce courts! When love of God is unappreciated and not repaid by a creature, life's darkest hour is experienced. When man, the creature, shows no appreciation for God, the Creator, we have the greatest tragedy possible.

Today, one of Advent's steps to Christmas affords us opportunity to return gratitude and to make reparation to God, to thank Him for the many blessings and benefits, and to repair the harm we have done by unrequited love.

Christmas affords us an occasion to make a gift of love to God and neighbor by trying to become more aware and conscious of our gifts and opportunities. Let us take this boundless love bestowed upon us in the scene of the Holy Nativity and give thanks to God for the depths of love He has given to us, and let us meditate upon the things for which we should be thankful.

Prayer

Jesus, take our hearts today and purify them in the fire of Your love so that no stain of hatred or enmity may be present to us. Teach us to be conscious of the insignificant little courtesies of life, that we may ever be grateful for Your love. You who live and reign with the Father in the unity of the Holy Spirit, God, forever and ever. Amen.

Tuesday of the Second Week of Advent: Our Lady and a Changing World

The feasts of Our Lady coming in Advent afford us an opportunity to think of the part womankind should play in the ever-present drama of life, for Mary is the model of all Christian womanhood. Women are endowed by the Creator with fine sensibilities and a most noble love. They are meant to be the inspiration of men. If the ideal of womankind is high, if she is exalted in men's estimation, if she is loved for her virtue, then the opportunity for good that is afforded mankind is tremendously great.

Paganism degraded womanhood and robbed her of her native dignity with which the Creator had endowed her. Mary's advent into the world, bringing the Savior of mankind, changed all that. She is "our tainted nature's solitary boast."[36] But alas, the new days of paganism are with us. This time again, the sad opportunity is afforded women to step down. A changing world in the guise of emancipation offers womankind an opportunity to lower her standards, to degrade her dignity, to debase her prerogatives for childbearing and motherhood.

---

[36] This line is taken from "The Virgin," by William Wordsworth. The entire poem is printed below.

Mother! whose virgin bosom was uncrost
With the least shade of thought to sin allied.
Woman! above all women glorified,
Our tainted nature's solitary boast;
Purer than foam on central ocean tost;
Brighter than eastern skies at daybreak strewn
With fancied roses, than the unblemished moon
Before her wane begins on heaven's blue coast;
Thy image falls to earth. Yet some, I ween,
Not unforgiven the suppliant knee might bend,
As to a visible Power, in which did blend
All that was mixed and reconciled in thee
Of mother's love with maiden purity,
Of high with low, celestial with terrene!

William Wordsworth, "The Virgin." Poetry Foundation, Accessed May 14, 2022, https://www.poetryfoundation.org/poems/45563 /the-virgin.

The Church has through the centuries watched over and guided the noble prerogatives of womankind, not because the Church bestowed these sacred rights, but because she preserves what has been restored through Our Lady and the Redemption. When woman is an ideal, man is, strictly speaking, a builder of the spirit. He builds within himself the great edifice of a spiritual character where the Holy Spirit dwells as in a temple. When woman is an ideal, men build homes, and children are received as the hope of a better world. The boy is looked up to so that he will carry on and build again as did his father, and the girl is cherished as the sweet daughter and mirror of the wife whose inward beauty grows more graceful with the passing years.

But the new paganism is threatening again! It is, of course, always in the name of freedom that freedom is abused. In the name of emancipation women are to be freed from the very duties that make them beautiful with a lasting beauty—motherhood and sharing in creation!

Women are meant to be builders, too, in the strictest sense of the term. They are the heart of the home. It is through them that men learn to live and to love great ideals and to build character. It is through the mother, definitely closer to the child than any other living human, that young habits and fine characters are formed. Women are the cornerstone of civilization in this respect. They are the hope of the world! "The hand that rocks the cradle rules the world."[37]

Anyone who calls himself a Christian and a follower of Christ must think often of the Blessed Mother of our Blessed Savior who was closest to Him all through the years that led up to Calvary. Anyone who respects women must know that it was Mary's role in Christian history to place women on the high pedestal they now enjoy. Anyone who has forebodings regarding the changes in our modern world will go to Mary and fervently pray that the rights, spiritual rights, of women be preserved, that they become modern Bethlehems in which Christ comes to dwell and not worldly inns that refuse children's birth.

None of us can live through a social revolution and come out of it unchanged ourselves. The world changing simply means that men and women of our day are changing. We must hold fast to Christian ideals, particularly the ideal of womankind as it comes to us from our Savior and from His Blessed Mother. If we lose this ideal, if women degrade themselves, they are not meeting, as we would have them meet, the challenge of a pagan world. They are succumbing!

---

[37] The closing lines of the poem, "The Hand that Rocks the Cradle is the Hand that Rules the World," by William Ross Wallace (1819–81).

They are delivering themselves to the enemies of Christian civilization. They are undoing the work of Redemption. They are despising Our Lady. That is unthinkable! Women are the builders of a better and a more secure world, where men may live as brothers because they have a common Father and a Blessed Mother.

Prayer

Our Lady of the hills and the valleys, look down from your throne in heaven and intercede with God in our behalf. As we live in a vale of tears preparing for the day when we may ascend the hill of heaven, pray for us, O Mary, that we may be worthy of the promises of Christ.

Intercede with God, that we may in imitation of you, follow Jesus along the way, though it be sorrowful out to the clear blue of the day, all the way up the hill, like you, to Calvary. We are sinners, like Magdalene. Accept us into your company. Few of us are like John, the beloved disciple; none of us is like you. Teach us to love Calvary and to see the sweet wood of the cross upon which hangs the Redeemer and our hope for eternal life. We ask this through Our Lord Jesus Christ, your son, who lives and reigns with the Father in the unity of the Holy Spirit, God, forever and ever. Amen.

Wednesday of the Second Week of Advent: The Dignity of Man

The Church celebrates the Feast of the Immaculate Conception in the United States of America as a holy day of obligation. The bishops of our country have dedicated our nation to the protection of Our Lady under this title. Fittingly is this so, for in the Declaration of Independence we read: "We hold these truths to be self-evident, that all men are created equal, that they are endowed by their Creator with certain inalienable rights, that among these are life, liberty, and the pursuit of happiness." Hence our Founding Fathers made clear their belief in the Creator and in the fact that He has endowed us with rights and liberties. These rights and liberties come from God. We are dependent upon God for them and not upon any State. God gives them; the State can only—and must—protect them.

The bishops of the United States, in one of their recent statements, made it clear that there could be no peace in the world until nations agree on the true nature of man, namely, that man has a dignity consisting in the fact that man is a creature of God and not a creature of the State.

The doctrine of the Immaculate Conception clearly identifies for Catholics the doctrine of the dignity of man.

It was Mary's privilege to have been conceived without sin. That privilege was given to no other human being. And God, in bestowing this renowned privilege upon one of His creatures, paved the way for the Redemption of man through His only-begotten Son who was to be born of this same Virgin Mother.

This privilege of Mary goes very deep into God's plans for all mankind. By the teaching of the Redemption and of Mary's Immaculate Conception, we are made aware of the fact that man is no machine—he is not a mere composition of matter that passes back into the earth. Man has a value other than his human existence. He has dignity apart from his ability to labor and to store up material wealth. Man is a creature of God composed of body and soul and made to the image and likeness of his Creator. Man has faculties of soul, intellect, and free will, which are to be trained according to their true ends and purposes. They are spiritual faculties and are meant for man's knowing and loving God. The solution to the world's crisis today rests in the answer to the question: are we men or are we beasts? There can be no peace until there is an agreement upon man's true dignity, for man is God's creature and not the State's! He is soul as well as body.

The world's excitement, its greed for wealth, its love for inordinate pleasure, its love for speed and distraction is not just an external quality of our times. It has become intrinsic to who we are all too often! This spirit of the world has seeped down into the very souls of men. It is not just the plane or the train of our age that speeds, but our minds and our souls! As haste is the death of devotion, so too, do greed, distraction, and pleasure spell death to those who should be devoted to the things of the soul. The noise of the world is too great a distraction to many who should spend moments of prayer and make an examination of conscience before God's Eucharistic Presence in some quiet little chapel. The spirit of the world is not the spirit of those who are inspired by the doctrine of the Redemption and the teaching of the Immaculate Conception. For they who are cognizant of man's dignity know that they were created not for the amassing of wealth for the State, but for the purpose of living for God here, and enjoying the Beatific Vision for all eternity!

Today, if men would return to a belief in their true nature, to a belief in their soul and its immortality, if they would have a continuation and preservation of their inalienable rights, they must return to the Creator from whom these rights came. There can be no peace until all mankind recognizes its true dignity.

Does not Mary, Virgin most venerable, remind us of this very thing! All is not yet lost, even though God "seems" so far away. Like a mother, who reassures her children, Mary reminds us that God is very close to souls who are close to His Mother. We should resolve to cherish the Virgin most venerable, and to pray always to live according to our true dignity, for God made us just a little less than the angels.

Prayer

Mary, you are all fair and there is no stain in you. We salute you as "our tainted nature's solitary boast" and we sing to you the sweet angel's song of "Ave Maria"—Hail Mary, full of grace, the Lord is with thee, blessed art thou among women and blessed is the fruit of thy womb, Jesus.

Holy Mary, Mother of God, pray for us sinners, now and at the hour of our death. Amen.

Thursday of the Second Week of Advent: Peace and Prayer

The Pope speaks to the world each Christmas eve. His message always carries a plea to all men to return to the ways of Christ, to the paths of peace.

Some years ago there appeared a very dramatic and eloquent picture of our Pope surrounded by his people outside the Vatican walls, praying in the bombed City of Rome. The caption read, "the Pope comes to the people." Indeed, the Holy Father is ever with the people. The shepherd is ever with his flock. It is we, the people, who have strayed from the fold and wandered down the avenues of the world away from the beacon light of the eternal city to the devious paths of sin and war.

Said Pope Pius: "We confide more in the help of your prayers than we do in the ability of the wisest statesmen and the valor of the most courageous combatant. Before God, prayer is more powerful than an arm of steel and bronze." This is the essence of the Holy Father's message that comes each Christmas time. It is the age-old teaching which has weathered every storm against faith and morals down through the centuries. It is the only solution to the ills of the world, and its formula must be applied to each individual soul before the cure is wrought.

The words of the Holy Father are broadcast each Christmas eve. They ring out over the world like the voice of the angels at Bethlehem. But as at Bethlehem, so in our own cities, there are ears that hear not, for they are not attuned to the voice of God. It is for these and for ourselves that we must pray. "For if today you hear His voice," says the Psalmist, "harden not your hearts."[38]

---

[38] Psalm 94:8.

In this Advent season wisely and most appropriately comes the feast of our blessed Lady, under her title, the Immaculate Conception. It is this doctrine that teaches us the true dignity of our nature. While hatreds and bombings only intensify the evil of human nature, prayer and a consideration of the virtues of Mary serve to lift us up above the earth to contemplate the fact that we are born for a high destiny. "Once and only once did God create a soul that was never even for an instant defiled with the slightest sin; once and only once did God create a soul that was as pure at the instant of conception as it is now in heaven; once and only once did He relax the stern judgment on our race and clothe a soul with original justice and sanctity and innocence and grace superabounding, with attributes of ineffable grandeur—a soul in which the Almighty could turn to gaze upon with pleasure when weary of the deformity which sin had stamped upon mankind," thus Canon Sheehan reminds us of Mary's dignity.

When man loses faith, he is left to view himself simply as a highly trained animal. There is then nothing sacred. There is no purpose to life. There is no hope for tomorrow's world. When faith remains and man sees himself a sinner fallen from grace, but yet with a high destiny as seen in the light of the doctrine of the Immaculate Conception, then there is high reason to hope and strive and pray for a better world. May American Catholics prove worthy of the cross that is being laid upon their shoulders as they have been dedicated to Our Lady.

Prayer

Mary Immaculate, in this Advent season, when the heavens rejoice, we your earthly clients lift up our voices in prayer. When our soul's craft rocks like a ship distressed upon the stormy seas of life, intercede with your divine Son in our behalf that we may be made worthy of the promises of Christ! Our Lady, Star of the Sea, pray for us!

Friday of the Second Week of Advent: Christmas and Children

Many years ago a little girl wrote a letter to the editor of a newspaper. The letter was among many received daily, but it got immediate attention and inspired a beautiful reply. So worthy and beautiful, indeed, that each year on Christmas Eve the *New York Sun* reprints this letter of the editor to the little Virginia who has grown with the years.[39]

The little girl, it seems, had believed in Santa Claus for a long time, and her firm belief was being shaken by

---

[39] "Yes, Virginia, there is a Santa Claus," *The New York Sun*, Editorial, September 21, 1897.

some of her cold and less imaginative companions. The editor's reply is a classic. "Virginia, your little friends are wrong. They have been affected by the skepticism of a skeptical age. They do not believe unless they see. They think that nothing can be which is not comprehensible by their little minds. All minds, Virginia, whether they be men's or children's, are little. In this great universe of ours, man is a mere insect, an ant in his intellect as compared with the boundless world about him, as measured by the intelligence capable of grasping the whole of truth and knowledge. Yes, Virginia, there is a Santa Claus," the editor continues. "He exists as certainly as love and generosity and devotion exist and you know that they abound and give to your life its highest beauty and joy. Alas how dreary would be the world if there were no Virginias. There would be no childlike faith, then, no poetry, no romance to make tolerable this existence. We would have no enjoyment except in sense and sight. The eternal light with which childhood fills the world would be extinguished. . . .

"The most real things in the world are those that neither children nor men can see. Nobody can conceive or imagine all the wonders there are unseen and unseeable in the world. . . . Only faith, fancy, poetry, love, and romance can push aside that curtain and view and picture the supernal beauty and glory beyond. Is it all real? Ah, Virginia, in all this world there is nothing else real and abiding."

The editor's lines live on, not because he proved anything about childhood's Santa, but because he conveyed so well the spirit of Christmas.

Children enjoy Christmas most of all because they are carefree and mostly because they are innocent. This world does take its toll on even the most sacrosanct. It dims the luster of our first fervor. We need acts of faith, hope, and charity to carry us on. Yet at Christmas time we come back closer to the joys of childhood because we come back to the infant Babe of Bethlehem whom Mary brings to us.

A priest was walking along the busy and thronged thoroughfare of Forty-second street in New York City as crowds were milling to and fro, when his eye caught sight of a man with a large placard suspended across his chest reading, "atheist." The priest passed very close to him. In fact, as he passed he looked directly into his eyes. The man said: "Father, here it is," holding aloft a paper, "written guarantees, there's no life hereafter." The priest with a kindly look passed on and thought to himself—a man speaking so courteously and addressing him as Father could hardly be an atheist. He remembered him at Mass as he spoke the words of consecration over the Host that God might bring the joy of Christmas faith to this man's strange and lonely heart—that he might be a child again, a child of God.

May our hearts be such this Christmas Day. Though the nations may be feverishly rearming and testing new weapons, may we this Christmas say thankfully, "Glory to God in the highest and on earth peace to men of good will."

Prayer

Little Jesus, with hearts full of faith and childlike simplicity we come today to pray for all those hearts which, like the inn of Bethlehem, refuse to open and receive You. Come into our hearts, Jesus, inflame them with Your love and make of them an eternal dwelling place for Your glory and our peace. You who live and reign with the Father in the unity of the Holy Spirit, God, forever and ever. Amen.

Saturday of the Second Week of Advent: Honor Your Mother

Next to the Godhead, Father, Son, and Holy Spirit, every Catholic cherishes a fond devotion to the Blessed Mother of God.

This devotion is really a part of our lives. That is to say, we grew up with it! As children we were attached to an earthly mother, and by her tender care and solicitude we were taught at her knee to pray to God's heavenly Mother, and to say: "Hail Mary, full of grace—pray for us sinners." Whenever our little minds attempted to comprehend the dignity of Mary, we always associated her with what was best in our own mothers.

We judge the unknown in terms of the known. As children we thought of God's Mother in terms of our own mothers. Hence, we gradually came to picture Mary as containing all the beautiful traits of earth's finest mothers. We saw mothers who kept nightly vigil over sickbeds, we saw their utter sacrifice as they wiped away sweat from fevered brows and soothed parched lips with moistened linen. Thus, we began to understand a little better the sufferings of Mary, God's Mother, at the foot of the cross. We noted that earthly mothers never spoke of self, never seemed to ask anyone to share their aches and pains. Thus, gradually we learned the lessons of Christian patience and forbearance.

We always associated Mary with the best of earthly mothers, for we pictured the Mother of God as the epitome of all that was best in motherhood.

Then came the dawn of further knowledge and an increase of grace, as we were instructed in revealed things. We were taught that Mary was singularly privileged above all other mothers—that she was immaculately conceived. Thus, it was we learned the meaning of the Church's doctrine of the Immaculate Conception. And then we thought of Mary not as our imagination would have painted her, but as God made her according to His own eternal designs: immaculately conceived, born without even the slightest stain of original sin and preserved by His all-holy grace, spotless and immaculately pure forever!

It was fittingly so, for how could God's Mother be dishonored by sin? God would never permit anything to come between Him and His Mother, which is just another way of saying that He preserved her from all stain by the foreseen merits of the Redemption. Let us honor our celestial Mother, calling to mind her most exalted spot as the greatest creature in the whole of the universe, and recall the honor that redounds to us and that we must live up to. She, the greatest of creation, calls us her very own children.

Prayer

To Our Lady, today, we may pray and say—

O Mary, immaculately conceived without sin, we pray you by all the virtues you possess to intercede for us that we may save our immortal souls. When the weakness of the Fall of our first parents is evident in our nature, and we are prone to evil, protect us and lead us back to God. When the darkness of sin overshadows our path, guide our footsteps. O most holy Mother, your body and your Immaculate Conception remind us of the beautiful monstrance to which the people of our churches contribute their gold and precious treasures of earth. For as Christ, the Babe of Bethlehem, is raised to bless our hearts, those who gave these things can say, "I helped in the benediction." Mary, your body was the resting place of Jesus Christ. Like a beautiful vessel of gold that enshrines its God, your holy abode was foreseen by the Creator from all eternity and was prepared and preserved from all stain and all blemish that it might raise up over all the world Him who is at once your Son and Redeemer—our Lord and Savior, Jesus Christ. You are truly a vessel of gold—house of God—gate of heaven at Christmas time.

Mother of the Savior, we honor God by recalling the spotless dignity of your Immaculate Conception. We pray that we may really be convinced of the fact that humanity is not so much "fallen" as it is "redeemed," that we are not so prone to evil that we cannot be uplifted and become filled with the spirit of God's grace. Do you, Mary, remind us again and again, whenever the tide of human passion rises like a mountainous sea—to look up—to see Christ and you—and to say: "Jesus, help. Mary, pray?"

O Mary, conceived without sin, pray for us who have recourse to you.

Third
Week of Advent

Third Sunday of Advent:
Joy and Peace

"The Jews sent from Jerusalem priests and Levites to John, to ask him: Who art thou? And he confessed, and did not deny: and he confessed: I am not the Christ. And they asked him: What then? Art thou Elias? And he said: I am not. Art thou the Prophet? And he answered: No. They said therefore unto him: Who art thou, that we may give an answer to them that sent us? What sayest thou of thyself? He said: I am the voice of one crying in the wilderness: Make straight the way of the Lord, as said the prophet Isaias. And they that were sent, were of the Pharisees. And they asked him, and said to him: Why then baptizest thou, if thou be not the Christ, nor Elias, nor the Prophet? John answered them, saying: I baptize with water; but there hath stood one in the midst of you, whom you know not; he it is, who shall come after me, who is preferred before me; the latchet of whose shoe I am not worthy to loose. These things were done in Bethania beyond the Jordan, where John was baptizing."[40]

The first word of the Mass of Gaudete Sunday, read in every Catholic church this morning, sounds the keynote of our faith. It is the Latin word, *gaudete*, which, being translated, means *rejoice.*

It is a striking paradox that the religion of the cross is at one and the same time the religion of joy. The solution of this paradox lies essentially in the fact that Christianity is a religion of love, and in this world love and sorrow are linked by a mysterious partnership. Christianity is no worshiper of pain, nor is asceticism an offering to a pain-loving God as if life and health were not God's good gifts. Much rather is Christianity a form of love, and love, being the root of joy, it follows that the practice of the Christian religion gives joy not in spite of its cross but rather as its natural consequence. For we are taught from earliest childhood as an elementary truth that man is on this earth for the one end of perfecting himself in the love of God. We know likewise that only through labor, pain, and sacrifice is love perfected. Pope Leo XIII, of happy memory, makes clear this point when he states that "Christianity has no

---

[40] John 1:19–28.

mission to eliminate labor, pain, and suffering from this world, but only to transmute them."

In his encyclical letter on the "Rosary and the Social Question,"[41] this great Pope and leader of Christendom speaks of the Sorrowful Mysteries of the Rosary as a means of correcting the false impressions of the world, namely, that suffering is repugnant and whatever is painful or harmful must be escaped. He goes on to state that "a great number of men are thus robbed of that peace and freedom of mind which remains the reward of those who do what is right undismayed by the perils or troubles that may be encountered in so doing. Rather do worldlings dream of a chimeric civilization in which all that is unpleasant shall be removed and all that is pleasant shall be supplied. For by this passionate and unbridled desire of living a life of pleasure the minds of men are weakened, and if they do not entirely succumb, they become demoralized and miserably cower and sink under the hardships of the battle of life."

With this fundamental truth, namely, that all joy is purchased at the price of sorrow and the crown of heaven

---

[41] Pope Leo XIII, *Laetitiae sanctae* (Sept. 8, 1893). Pope Leo XIII wrote on the Rosary twelve times during his pontificate, almost every year, such was his powerful devotion and promotion of the Rosary.

won by the warriors who carry a cross, does Holy Mother Church impress us this Gaudete Sunday. The penitential colors of Advent today give way to the rose-colored vestments of joy. For "joyfulness is the life of man and a never failing treasure of holiness," says Holy Writ.[42] The solemn notes of preparation give way to the jubilant sound of organ music. Holy Mother Church chooses as her liturgical station today the tomb of the Prince of the Apostles in the Basilica of St. Peter in Rome, where today we hear the only voice of peace and joy in a world that verges upon war. Here today is heard the echo of Peter's voice in the person of his successor, who is teaching us the lesson of Gaudete Sunday, namely, that all joy and peace can come only through Christ who first suffered and died before entering into His glory.

Isaias, the Prophet of the Advent season, reminds us again that the Church is the "City of strength."[43] We, her children, gather in spirit today around the tomb of the humble fisherman in the Vatican Basilica. Only here in the Church of Christ can we find strength, only here can we find peace and joy in a sickened and depressed world.

---

[42] Sirach 30:23.
[43] Isaiah 26:1.

In the Advent Gospel of the Mass we read, "There hath stood one in the midst of you, whom you know not."[44] How applicable are these words of St. John the Baptist to the present day! Christ stands in the midst of this civilization. His Mystical Body is the Church. His Vicar is Peter's successor, whose voice emanates from the Vatican today as Mass is celebrated over the tomb of Peter. In the midst of a world that is seeking joy and peace, Christ stands awaiting the visit of nations. On this day of Advent, God grant that "the peace of Christ in the reign of Christ"[45] may take hold of the earth that "our sorrow may be turned into joy."[46]

Prayer

Dear Savior of men, teach me to place all my confidence not in the wisdom of men, but in the foolishness of the cross. Alas, men promise material joy and they give us but ashes of defeat. You have promised us a cross, which is but the prelude to the crown. Teach us, blessed Savior, that there is peace of soul, joy of spirit, and eternal repose and contentment only in the Christian way of life. Grant us the grace to follow You on the *Via Dolorosa*, that it

---

[44] John 1:26.
[45] Pope Pius XI, *Ubi Arcano Dei Consilio* (On the Peace of Christ in the Kingdom of Christ), (December 23, 1922).
[46] John 16:20.

may become the cause of our joy. Our Lady of Sorrows, pray for us!

Monday of the Third Week of Advent: Christmas and the Home

G. K. Chesterton, in one of his essays entitled, *The Spirit of Christmas*, tells of the hustle and bustle, the buying and selling that accompanies this great feast day of the Church's calendar. He distinguishes between the accidental and essential meaning of the feast. Gift giving should not make us wary of losing the meaning of Christmas. Rather, the danger lies in that one cling only to gift giving's external and commercial appeal and that we may lose sight of the essential meaning of Christmas: "Christmas is built upon a beautiful and intentional paradox; that the birth of the homeless should be celebrated in every home."

Essentially Christmas is the feast day of the home and the child.

We shall celebrate Christmas this year, it is true, by attending holy Mass, by prayers at the crib, and by singing the Christmas carols. But shall we have the true spirit of Christmas? It is true, please God, we shall have Christ with us and our love for His Blessed Mother will be warm, tender, wise, and noble. But any one of us who gives reflection and thought to the world in which we live realizes how far this world is today from the true spirit of Christmas. A world of unrest, threatened by war, means a temporary disrupting of our homes. It means for so many young men and women a temporary postponement of marriage, a delay for home building and the rearing of children. Instead of the sweet innocent play and laughter of children, who give to Christmas its sacred tone and true spirit, we have the roar of motors in the air, the quiet steady smoke of factories throughout the land producing war materials. Off in the distance can be heard the thunder of mighty cannon and the testing of atomic weapons.

Great are the upheavals of war. Among them are the moral dangers to young men, the lonely hours of young women, the new inducement for women to forget home life and take to industry, the lack of care on the part of parents for children who must be sheltered in nurseries. This can be our world at Christmas, and while we realize these dangers, we must pray for peace and for a victory with justice to all. We cannot be like the melancholy Dane and say, "The time is out of joint, O cursed spite, that ever I was born to set it right."[47] No, we must pray for the real, true, genuine spirit of Christmas—for homes, for children.

---

[47] *Hamlet*, Act I, Scene 5, ll, 188–89.

For Christmas is the season of the home and the child. In these two notes are found its true spirit. He who created the world came into it in the Incarnation and His own received Him not. As Chesterton remarked, He is "homeless at home," the great God of heaven and earth becomes a Babe in order to teach us humility. The omnipotent God came wrapped in the weakness of swaddling bands. He gave to us the blessings of Christmas: homes and children.

There are houses today with nobody in them because now, as of old, there are men who refuse to admit the Mother and Child. There are hearts today without God in them because they are proud and selfish like the keepers of the inn, and they refuse to admit the Child of heaven, the incarnate One of Bethlehem. There are Catholic souls today who refuse to accept the Babe in the form of the Eucharist because their lives would have to be remodeled and reverted to the lowliness of belief. This devoutly to be wished for transformation would make them humble enough to see their foolish pride and to accept the humble Child.

We pray today for the victory promised through her, the Immaculate One, who will "crush the head of the serpent." We pray for that spiritual victory which will give America the true spirit of Christmas. We pray for the welcoming and loving of children and home to overpower our hearts and renew our souls. In short, may God give us the grace of living out the true meaning of Christmas.

Prayer

O Virgin Mother of the Babe of Bethlehem, we pray you to intercede for America in our behalf and for spiritual victory. In our homes we pray that God may send angels to guide us and to make of them sanctuaries. We pray to God, through you, that He give to America a love for the wholesome things of life, to let us see that there can be no nation unless there be homes with children in whom there is the true spirt of God and of Christmas. We ask this through Our Lord Jesus Christ, your son, who lives and reigns with the Father in the unity of the Holy Spirit, God, forever and ever. Amen.

Tuesday of the Third Week of Advent: Fear Not

Hours of mental anguish can be transmuted into hours of accomplishment by the alchemy of love if the pain is offered both in atonement for sins and in reparation for offenses committed against God. This can be done by individuals in pain and by nations as a whole when the world is suffering the agony of war and witnessing some of the darkest hours of all human history. Many a gold star in a service flag denotes the sacrifice of mothers who have given sons to the cause, and of families that have lost the shepherding hand of a kindly father.

When the moon hides the face of the sun, it is an interesting phenomenon of nature to witness as the earth is darkened by shadow, but there is no one nowadays who is fearful of such an occurrence, for we have learned to know that it is only a passing eclipse and that the sun will soon give its light to cheer the heart of man. We know that the moon is only a satellite receiving its light from the sun, and after a few fleeting moments the sun will be seen shining in all its brilliance, giving to earth its benediction of light and heat without which we could not live.

Thus, when the darkness of war casts a shadow across the earth, eclipsing for the moment the brightness of peace, some are fearful, for they lack the assurance and light of faith which is a comfort in times of darkest mental anguish. They have grown accustomed to living according to the way of the world. When the lights go out all over the world there is no further hope for them beyond this vale of shadows. It is not so, however, with the faithful. Through prayer and a deep abiding belief, the man of faith continues to place his trust not in earthly princes but in an all-provident God. He is aware that man and not God is accountable for the woes of the world and that they are caused by sin! Thus it is that he offers the agony of heart and the distressing moments of war in prayerful attitude to the Almighty as atonement for his sins and those of mankind.

The man of faith, in whose heart is the grace of God, believes that Christ is the Light of the World. Although the darkness of evil on Calvary seemed to blacken out the divine light, yet the man of faith is aware that no human power, however strong, can long withstand divinity's hand.

The world's excitement, its race to arm men with the weapons that kill, its greed for money, and its lust for pleasure have left a deep mark upon our day and age. Only spiritual remedies can go deep enough to effect a radical change, and only spiritual leadership can help cure our present ills.

The speed of our day with its love for distraction has seeped way down into the very hearts and souls of men. It is not just something characteristic of the day. It is almost an intrinsic quality of our hearts. It is not the plane or atom that speeds. It is the heart of man that has learned how speedily to kill. Spiritual ideals inculcated again in human hearts alone can root out the present evils and give the plan for a better, safer, and a more peaceful world. A quiet visit to the sick, a prayer uttered in a way-side chapel, a helping hand, an hour made holy before the Eucharistic King, a morning prayer, a fast broken only at the altar with the Eucharistic Lord—such as these must be learned by the children of men if a more peaceful life is to be lived by the followers of the Prince of Peace. This opportunity is offered each of us during this Advent season: to watch and pray with Christ and Mary and Joseph.

To inculcate in the minds of the faithful the need for prayer and sacrifice, the Church has set aside special days, called Ember Days, on which these should be practiced in thanksgiving to God for the gifts of nature, to teach men to make use of them in moderation, and to assist the needy. We should prepare and resolve to perform some special act in the spirit of the Ember triduum during Advent, which begins tomorrow.

Prayer

Lord Jesus Christ, You promised not to leave us orphans and You have given us a Father on earth in our Holy Father to guide our steps and inspire our hearts. Today we pray for him through the intercession of Our Lady, Queen of Peace. Give strength to him and abundant grace to give this world spiritual aid. You who live and reign with the Father in the unity of the Holy Spirit, God, forever and ever. Amen.

Ember Wednesday of Advent: Purposeful Sacrifice

The Church asks us to accept sacrifice voluntarily and to consecrate our pains by placing them at the foot of the crucifix. This is the pattern for Advent as well as for Lent, the Church's two predominant penitential seasons.

There is a question as old as man himself, spoken in as many languages as there are peoples in the world, and yet one that still is asked in quest of an answer: "Why does God send me suffering?" Sometimes the question is presented in the form of a problem: "Why should the good suffer while the bad and the wicked seem to prosper?" The real problem might be summed up by asking "How can we reconcile suffering and sin with God's goodness?" Or, again, "Why should God the Father freely create a world and creatures that would fall away and require a Redemption in the sufferings of His only begotten Son?" We shall endeavor to seek a satisfactory answer to the problem in our meditation this Advent day.

Our holy faith alone can answer these questions. Unaided reason is unavailing. Search as far and as long as we will, the answer still eludes us, unless we turn to faith and revelation. We have to look to the teachings of Christ! The human mind can plumb no further the mysteries of

God, but faith in God and our Lord Jesus Christ enables us to rise superior to the limitations of finite reasoning and see through the mists and shadows the unerring wisdom and benevolent will of God. That is sufficient for our quest. This was the course Christ outlined for us when He walked the earth in human form. He did not attempt to extirpate evil from the kingdom of the world at large. He left that for time to come. Instead He preached to sinners the way of penance. He preached to Pharisees, though He knew they were whited sepulchers with stony hearts. He tolerated them to the very end. This is the attitude of the Church and her faithful members. Endure both the wicked and the good—"suffer both to grow until the harvest; and in the time of the harvest I will say to the reapers: Gather up first the cockle, and bind it in bundles to burn, but the wheat gather ye into my barn."[48]

We should remember, too, that God's goodness is not infringed upon by the possibility of evil. When man has rightly used that which God has given him—and man always has sufficient grace to overcome evil—then God rewards him. God, therefore, fulfills all justice.

We cannot refrain from referring to a beautiful story written on the problem of evil in the world. The novel

---

[48] Matthew 13:30.

was written by the late Owen Francis Dudley, entitled *The Shadow on the Earth*. In the narrative the author depicts two characters: one is a cripple who has lost the use of his limbs through an accident in the Alpine Mountains; the other, a man who has become a confirmed atheist and who tries to convince the suffering companion that there is no God, and if there were, He certainly would not permit him to suffer.

The story is beautifully worked out to a hopeful and happy conclusion, showing the childlike faith and simplicity of the cripple, whose sufferings served only to confirm his faith, whilst the man who was more prosperous from a worldly viewpoint, grew cynical and depressed. The spirit of the cripple was ennobled and uplifted by suffering. The shadow on the earth is the cross, and this is his hope and his salvation! One man lost his ability of going from place to place on earth through physical handicap; the other lost his faith which would have given him ability to climb toward heaven and would have pierced the clouds and given understanding of the problem of suffering.

The cross of Christ is indeed "a yoke that is sweet and a burden that is light."[49] It is a blessed shadow on the earth, but the shadow of the all-protecting hand of the all-wise

---

[49] Matthew 11:30.

and provident God. For just as a cloud in the heavens sometimes obscures the sun, and leaves the earth darkened and shadowed, so oft-times a cross darkens the light of happiness in our own lives and temporarily closes out the sight of an all-wise God. Though we may temporarily fail to enjoy the shadowy clouds and raindrops and the dew-drops of earth, we realize that they give growth to the things that gladden our hearts and eventually become our food. Likewise, if it were not for the pain of mothers repeopling the earth with hearts of children—if it were not for the pains and crosses of life, we could never enjoy the joys and felicities that make life worth living! The answer to all our sorrows and the answer to the so-called problem of evil lies in a deeper faith and a firmer trust in the goodness of God. It lies in repeating the prayer of the suffering Christ: "Father, if Thou wilt, remove this chalice from Me: but yet, not My will, but Thine be done."[50] Sacrifice, then, when purposeful, has real meaning and worth, for it leads to the peace of soul which we are seeking through Christ, our Lord.

Prayer

Dear Jesus, when my life seems to have a greater share of thorns than rose petals, teach me the lesson of Gethsemani,

---

[50] Luke 22:42.

where You accepted the chalice through prayer to Your heavenly Father.

My will is weak, my resolution is not firm, but strengthen them and teach me the ways and means to kneel and pray even in the darkness of Gethsemani and Calvary, that I may grow to love sacrifice as you, my Captain, do. You who live and reign with the Father in the unity of the Holy Spirit, God, forever and ever. Amen.

Thursday of the Third Week of Advent: Peace through Christ

How shall godless men ever set this world aright? Often, these men seek peace by means of war, yet this is never the solution. The mighty men of the world rule simply by force and not by justice. True peace can only be won by the rulers of men if it is founded upon God as the Supreme Being and mankind as His brotherly children. If, therefore, a nation be godless, we cannot hope to find peace by aligning our cause to it. First we must seek the Kingdom of God and His justice and all else shall be added thereunto.

The peace of our hearts at Advent time must be a Christlike quest, for only in Christ shall we find a true foundation for our hopes. All else is fleeting and all too brief. The peace of Christ is permanent, delivered by prayer and won by sacrifice.

The peace of Christ is the peace of Christmas which follows the season of penitential Advent. The lesson of Gaudete Sunday, too, is that joy is purchased at the price of penance and heaven is won by the warriors who carry a cross.

The peace of Christ is not the peace of one nationality lording it over another because of a mightier army or a more powerful banking system. Alas, all such power, being founded upon very unstable bases, is bound to pass away. The peace of Christ, which is the fruit of justice, can be brought to pass only when the principles of the Master, found in the Gospels and enunciated by the Vicar of Christ, are practiced by all nations seeking our common end, namely, God's glory and man's eternal destiny. This end requires curtailment of selfish ends. It means a curbing of national pride when that pride oversteps its bounds by infringing upon the rights of other nations. Greed is the cancer that has eaten away at the very vitals of men and nations, and only the healing hand of the divine Physician can reach down and, getting at the cause of our troubles, cut it away. Human diplomacy and ingenuity can never restore peace unless it is based and founded upon God.

This brings us to the second much needed element in the attainment of peace, namely, prayer. Says the poet, "More things are wrought by prayer than this world dreams of,"[51] but prayer is not the fruit of a worldly generation. Prayer is man's inmost conversing with God. With the roar of cannon, with so much emphasis on man and so little emphasis on God, prayer becomes a forgotten instrument in the attainment of peace. For the spirit becomes secondary to the material in the life of a modern worldling until prayer, being neglected, becomes dead and buried.

Pope Pius XII promised France his understanding, sympathy, and encouragement in her struggle to recover from the war when he received the credentials of the French ambassador to the Holy See. It is comforting to read, too, the spiritual reflection of the ambassador, who said that since the expectations of earthly help had been vain France was now turning toward a more enduring source of comfort. The ambassador said that France "adheres to the peace of the Holy Father as so often invoked and defended." The French people, said the Holy Father, would find nowhere "a more prompt co-operation, a more intimate sympathy, a more sincere encouragement than from the common Father of all the faithful." Let us

---

[51] Idylls of the King. The Passing of Arthur, l. 415.

too turn to our spiritual ambassadors, the communion of saints, in helping us find that true peace after we have been caught in the trenches of sin for far too long, and find true life, true peace, and true happiness adoring the Divine Child in the manger this Christmas.

Prayer

Blessed Savior, you came into the world on Christmas Day to bring peace to all mankind, behold we, Your suppliant children, implore You to give us peace—the peace which the world cannot give, the peace of justice, the peace of charity, your true eternal peace which leads to everlasting life. You who live and reign with the Father in the unity of the Holy Spirit, God, forever and ever. Amen.

Ember Friday of Advent: Peace and Stars

In the windows in many homes the Christmas star of Bethlehem will be companioned by the gold star of the service flag. Side by side will appear the reminders of peace and war, of life and death. In a confused world men look for some blueprint that they might get started aright again, for some beam to set them back on their course, for some star with which to set their compass of life.

Today it is well-nigh Christmas again, the day on which was born the Prince of Peace. But, alas, the world knows no peace. It is confused beyond measure with threats of war, cold war, and class warfare.

Today the Church announces again the glad tidings of joy. In so doing, she acts not like a fool, who says, "All is well, all is well," when beneath there is a raging torrent of hatred and evil. No! The Church alone of all the institutions of our day is able to speak of peace, because she alone is the ambassador of the Prince of Peace. She bears His unchanging credentials.

The Church has experienced her Good Friday. Like a man who has survived a dreaded disease and, having once gone down to the valley of suffering, has built up a resistance to the germ, the Church in even a more salutary way than this has suffered her defeats in persecution and crucifixion and she will divinely survive all the hatreds of the world which breed wars and global holocausts.

Hence, only a divinely inspired institution like the Church of God can talk of peace in a world at war. What assurance can men give of sustained harmony among nations? Built upon the fallible word of man, treaties melt away like snowflakes once they fall upon the anvil fire of human perversity. Only upon the infallible truths of God revealed through His Church can we safely rest our future security, and so the bonded word of nations wedded in treaties of peace can only be of lasting value when rested upon the infallible truth of God and cemented through the Church's dispensation.

Men are confused as they talk of peace and continue plans for war, but the Church is calm. God's justice and peace must eventually reign. Hence the Church can speak of Christmas stars over Bethlehem and gold stars in our American homes at one and the same time without confusion. The Church can speak of resurrection even though it be Good Friday, for the Church is not of this world. Even while the world seems to be slipping from beneath her feet can she speak of Christ and God and peace eternal. The world shall pass away, but not so the eternal Mystical Spouse of Christ, not so all those members of that Mystical Body that share its life. To all mothers who bear in their hearts the gold star of a son's sacrifice the Church speaks of another Mother who brought life to the world beneath Bethlehem's starry skies, of another Mother who gave life and saw it die in crucifixion and then rise again in glory. So shall it be with all life that suffers defeat—if incorporated with the life of Christ, it shall rise again! The stars that were blue in loyalty and have now turned gold in undying death bear hope to mothers' hearts when viewed in the light of the heavens and Bethlehem's star.

Not confusion here, but order and peace of soul is the reward for all those who find their way to the crib and the feet of Christ.

Prayer

Babe of Bethlehem, guard us against the confused error of the world mistaking earthly possession for heavenly reward. Guide our lives by Your star. Surrounded by temptation, circumvented by worldliness, teach us to ordain all things to our eternal end—glory to God, peace to men of good will. You who live and reign with the Father in the unity of the Holy Spirit, God, forever and ever. Amen.

Ember Saturday of Advent: Fidelity to Christ

It was once reported to Alexander the Great that one of his soldiers had behaved cowardly in the face of an enemy. "What is your name?" the conquering Emperor asked the trembling soldier. "Alexander," the man answered. The Emperor then said to him: "Do you know that is my name, too? Either change your name or change your behavior."

How many, today, could be reproached with their repudiating Christ's principles and yet retaining the name of Christian. How many there are, today, who avow themselves followers of the Nazarene, but hardly live in accordance with the teachings of the Sermon on the Mount. They refuse to forgive as their Captain Christ forgave even His enemies as they nailed Him to a tree.

Since the days of the so-called Reformation the world has been trying to live on the patrimony of Christian culture while denying some of the foremost teachings of Christ. The world has tried the experiment of compromising norms—of being Christian without Christ. The distinctly Protestant notion that human nature is corrupt and that Christ's merits simply cover up the evils present in men's souls has found many a follower. The danger of such a belief is that it prompts men to look upon Christ as the scapegoat who was offered up for the sins of mankind as a satisfaction to the Eternal Father, forgetting that salvation requires man's co-operation. Redemption means an application of Christ's merits to our souls. But this requires a response on our part to God's grace.

In such a world where men wish to be known as Christian but refuse to obey the mandates of the Christian moral code there is great confusion and little contentment. This defection of the human mind and will has been in progress for so long a time that we have come to face a world that has lost faith in God, and consequently confidence in its fellow men.

The State has usurped the place of God, and man becomes a mere tool and pawn of tyrants. Humanity is asked to accept as the ideal order a State, the ruler of man's body and soul. Somewhere in this world there is the voice of Christ heard in His Vicar. He speaks not only to those who recognize him as the Vicar of Jesus Christ. He speaks to all the children of men who have need of his direction. The Pope places emphasis on the moral principles which alone will save the human race from destruction. He makes a plea for the rights of the individual man upon which all well-ordered society rests. He insists that the personal integrity of man must not be violated by any State. For these same rights and the dignity of man are granted not by any human power but are infused by God.

Thus, the Vicar of Christ pleads for fidelity to the Savior of the human race. The Pope is pleading with men for a return to Christian principles and a restoration of the natural law. Our modern world, while retaining the name of Christian, has done much to destroy the very foundations of Christian society.

We look today, then, not for a new philosophy of life nor a new economic theory. We look for no superman to lead us from a world threatened with destruction by wicked men. We look only up to God and pray that the words of His lawful representatives will be heeded, so that soon peace may reign in our land and in all the world, a peace with justice gained through fidelity to Christ. This should be our special intention on this Ember Day, for prayer can be our "widow's mite" in helping to obtain peace on earth which is the reward to men of good will.

Prayer

O Lord, inspire rulers and peoples with grace to see the errors of the past and to resolve to live the Christian life in the future. Heal the discord of nations. Grant that Your precious blood, shed for all mankind, may prompt their hearts to forgive and to build a world where love may reign again. You who live and reign with the Father in the unity of the Holy Spirit, God, forever and ever. Amen.

FOURTH WEEK OF ADVENT[52]

Sunday of the Fourth Week of Advent: Tune in Heaven

"In the fifteenth year of the reign of Tiberius Caesar, Pontius Pilate being governor of Judea, and Herod tetrarch of Galilee, and Philip his brother tetrarch of Iturea and the country of Trachonitis, and Lysanias tetrarch of Abilina: under the high-priests Annas and Caiphas: the word of the Lord came unto John the son of Zacharias, in the desert. And he came into all the country about the Jordan, preaching the baptism of penance for the remission of sins, as it is written in the book of the sayings of Isaias the Prophet: The voice of one crying in the wilderness:

---

[52] NB: The Fourth Week of Advent's length varies depending on the liturgical year. Note that whatever day Christmas Eve falls upon in this week will replace that day's liturgy.

Prepare ye the way of the Lord, make straight his paths. Every valley shall be filled, and every mountain and hill be brought low: the crooked shall be made straight, and the rough ways plain: and all flesh shall see the salvation of God."[53]

Holy Mother Church has thus far been teaching us to prepare for the Advent of Jesus by salutary fear, by inspired courage, by joyful peace, and now, as we stand almost at the threshold of the cave of Bethlehem, we are exhorted to prepare the way of the Lord by prayer and penance.

Those who wish to enter into the very presence of God must be holy. As the adage says, "fools rush in where angels fear to tread," a pertinent phrase Holy Mother Church adopts in urging us to do penance. On Gaudete Sunday we learned that all joy is purchased at the price of sorrow and the crown of heaven won only by a penitential carrying of a cross; this last Sunday of Advent, we see that all nature and life itself attest to the fact that mortification and penance are necessary.

The little seedling must be buried in the ground and die to self before it can bring forth the beauty of a rose and perfume a garden of earth. Students must assiduously apply themselves to the task at hand if they ever wish to communicate knowledge to others. Mothers must

---

[53] Luke 3:1–6.

endanger their lives in order to replenish the earth with babes that make for us a veritable heavenly nursery. Doctors must, by long vigils of study and work, prepare before they may be entrusted with the care of human bodies. Priests must be sanctified and grounded in learning so as to account themselves, as St. Paul tells us in the Advent Epistle, "as ministers of Christ and dispensers of the mysteries of God."[54] Only then are they to be entrusted with the care of immortal souls. In other words, in any life whatsoever, preparation is necessary and penance is the "divine" preparation. "Unless the seed falling into the ground die, itself remaineth alone, but if it die it beareth much fruit."[55] Unless we are willing to do penance and to prepare for Christ's coming, we cannot hope to be His disciples nor to find the journeying star that leads to His joyous crib.

St. Luke warns us in the Advent Gospel, "Prepare ye the way of the Lord, make straight his paths."[56] This preparation of penance is to be made, as St. John exemplified, by our actions, for actions speak louder than words.

---

[54] I Cor. 4:1.

[55] John 12:24–25.

[56] Luke 3:4.

When a distinguished visitor is announced at your door, do you not make it a point to be sure that you are prepared to meet him? Do you not take pains to see that the home is properly prepared and all is ready? Holy Mother Church announces all the more today: "The Lord is nigh; come, let us adore."[57] Christ the Lord is coming. He is nigh, even at your doorsteps. The prophets announced His coming, and yet even some of the Jews were unprepared. The Church announces again His Advent, and will it be said of you that "unto His own He came and His own received Him not"?[58] Are you preparing by penance for the arrival of the King? Is it not possible that you miss the sweet inspirations of God's grace unless you are "attuned" to God's message?

Picture in your mind's eye a person seated at a radio or a television set that is not tuned in to a station transmitting beautiful philharmonic music or even has the proper station on but has muted the sound altogether. Such a person misses entirely the program. Picture again a Catholic not at all solicitous about the penance of Advent nor the beautiful story being told by holy Mother Church. Such a one is not "attuned" to the spirit of the liturgy nor

---

[57] Antiphon for the Invitatory at Matins in the Divine Office. (NB: "Office of Readings" in the Liturgy of the Hours subsumed the hour entitled "Matins" in the Divine Office at this time.)
[58] John 1:11.

to the sweet whisperings of grace and God's inspirations in the soul, and he may entirely miss the message of Advent and the promptings of the Holy Spirit.

Members of Christ's Mystical Body, hearken to the "greatest story ever told" by the greatest mother of them all! The story is God's becoming man. The mother is the Catholic Church. Today she makes a last effort to enliven our faith, to increase our devotion and our preparation by penance for the coming of Jesus Christ. As a stimulus to our faith and devotion she asks us to look to the new crib of Bethlehem, to the altar, to the snow-white manger of a corporal where a golden chalice rests upon it. Perhaps, we have seen a nugget of gold when first mined from the earth. It is dark, grimy, and covered with dirt. Yet the miner who knows its value cherishes it, refines it, purifies and ennobles it, until one day it is returned to its proper state—shining, brilliant, pure gold! It is, then, perhaps, molded into a chalice or ciborium and, being consecrated to God's service, it holds the sacred species of the Body and Blood of Christ in the Eucharist. Likewise, our hearts are gold, and more precious indeed since redeemed by the blood of the Lamb of God. We should therefore endeavor to purify our hearts and souls during this holy season of Advent and to sanctify them by the reception of our divine Lord in Holy Communion. May our hearts be made into more purified, more refined, more ennobled chalices, the manger Christ wishes to rest on that holy day, and the same hearts be found all the more worthy to receive Christ when He shall come to us in the Blessed Eucharist on Christmas Day!

Prayer

Blessed Savior of men, the view of Calvary from afar is forbidding. The way of prayer and penance is not easy. There is only one way to Mount Calvary and that is to follow You, step by step. To look up the hill of Calvary takes great courage of heart—so give me the grace to stay close to You and accompany You each step of the journey. Bethlehem is but the first step to Calvary. Take me by the hand of grace and teach me to walk with Mary, that my life may be good and worthy of redemption. You who live and reign with the Father in the unity of the Holy Spirit, God, forever and ever. Amen.

Monday of the Fourth Week of Advent: Listen—God Speaks Softly

"Now in the sixth month the angel Gabriel was sent from God to a town of Galilee called Nazareth, to a virgin betrothed to a man named Joseph, of the house of David, and the virgin's name was Mary. And when the angel had come to her, he said: 'Hail, full of grace, the Lord is with thee. Blessed art thou among women.' When she had seen him she was troubled at his word, and kept pondering what manner of greeting this might be. And the angel said to her: 'Do not be afraid, Mary, for thou hast found grace with God. And behold thou shalt conceive in thy womb and shalt bring forth a son; and thou shalt call his name Jesus. He shall be great, and shall be called the Son of the Most High; and the Lord God will give him the throne of David his father, and he shall be king over the house of Jacob forever; and of his kingdom there shall be no end.'

"But Mary said to the angel, 'How shall this happen, since I do not know man?'

"And the angel answered and said to her: 'The Holy Spirit shall come upon thee and the power of the Most High shall overshadow thee; and therefore the Holy One to be born shall be called the Son of God. . . .'

"But Mary said: 'Behold the handmaid of the Lord; be it done to me according to thy word.' And the angel departed from her."[59]

This is the narrative of the Gospel according to St. Luke wherein we have the first singing of the Ave Maria by an

---

[59] Luke 1:26–38.

angel. A virgin takes up the beautiful strains and accepts the summons of grace. An invitation is given through an angel, and Mary is receptive and graciously accedes to God's will.

This story of the Annunciation is related not a one-time occurrence in human history, but repeats many times throughout the ages. Indeed, it happens as often as a new rational soul is conceived. In the life of every man and woman born into the world there is an annunciation of the angel of God. Rather, this annunciation occurs every time that God's grace is poured forth from heaven into any soul. All too often the story is very different from Mary's. Grace is spurned. Souls are not found in the attitude of prayer as was Mary. They are not on their knees. Their hearts are not as was the immaculate heart of Mary, attuned to the loving heart of God. The voice of the angel is drowned out by the noise of the world and the distractions of modern living.

During these Advent days God is sending His angel of grace to drop the seed of inspiration to Christian living into our hearts. We must till the soil by prayer and penance if the seed would take root. We must be on our knees, like Mary, and in the silence of our chamber, in reflection must we be found if the angel is to be heard above the tumultuous riot of noise and distraction which characterizes our day.

The important thing about the annunciation of Mary is that she heard in silence the invitation. She reflected and then *accepted*. Acceptance of God's inspiration depends on us. God never, never forces our wills! We are not conditioned by grace. We are free to refuse. Therein is the story of salvation.

God comes into the world as He did at Bethlehem and knocks upon the inn of human hearts. Angels like Gabriel are sent by God as His messengers from heaven. They give us the gravitation of heaven. They set a tugging or pulling of our hearts. They move us to good by gentle reminders and holy inspirations. But they never force our souls!

With every *annunciation*, it is sad to say, there is the possibility of a *renunciation* of grace. Acceptance requires the work of a good life and the practice of virtue. Hence, Advent penance and prayer are a prerequisite if we are to imitate Mary. Angels' songs are sweet to contemplate. Ave Marias are pleasant to hear. But we must do our part and add our share to the angels' task. We are men and women of flesh and blood and have been created just a little less than the angels. We must strive for perfection that we may be in a position like Mary to say: *Fiat mihi secundum verbum tuum*—"Be it done unto me according to thy word."

During this final week of preparation for Christmas, let our prayer be, "Speak, Lord, for thy servant heareth."[60] The Psalmist reminds us, "If, today, you hear His voice, harden not your heart."[61]

Christmas takes us back in memory to Bethlehem and to Nazareth. The story of Bethlehem is the tale of God's obedience. He was obedient to the will of the Father in assuming human form in order to placate divine justice. Mary continues the procession of divine love, she places her heart at the disposal of God's movements of grace. Without her obedience the angel's song would have been discordant. Without God's great act of humility in coming to Bethlehem, there would have been no Redemption. And without man's submission to God's will in imitation of Mary's response at Nazareth there can be no peace on earth.

Bethlehem or Nazareth is not an incident of history. It is repeated every time God comes to hearts that are opened to receive Him. In this year of grace as we prepare for Christmas we are making history. There is always an *annunciation*, for God gives grace to all creatures. Please and pray God, may there be less *renunciations!*

---

[60] 1 Samuel 3:10.

[61] Psalm 94:8.

Prayer

O Jesus, Savior of the world, who came to men in the weakness of a Babe, teach us that the greatest lessons are learned by humble souls. When the noise of the world would distract us, teach us to fall upon our knees, like humble shepherds and lowly fisher men. When angels' songs break the silence of our souls, help us to be like Mary, and to say, "Speak, Lord. Thy servant heareth. Be it done as Thou wilt." And lest my aspiration to higher things be but wishful thinking, help me, O Lord, to till the soil of my heart by prayer and penance, that my soul be receptive and the seed take root. You who live and reign with the Father in the unity of the Holy Spirit, God, forever and ever. Amen.

Tuesday of the Fourth Week of Advent: Christ Knocks

"Behold I stand at the gate and knock,"[62] says the Lord in the Apocalypse.

An artist has painted this scene. In the picture Christ stands before a door and raises His hand to knock upon it. The artist's little son, looking at the painting, said: "Daddy,

---

[62] Apocalypse 3:20.

there is a mistake in the picture." "What mistake?" asked the father. The boy answered: "There isn't any latch on the door to let the man in." "Son," replied the father, "what seems to be a mistake here, really shows the truth. That man is the Lord God. The door opens into the human heart. The key is on the inside. The door must be opened from the inside before our Lord is able to enter."

This little episode is so true that it makes a simple yet great teaching. The latch on the inside is our free will. God could have made, if He wished, a different kind of world than He actually made. He could have chosen to come otherwise than as a little weak Babe. He could have come as a powerful king. But He did not. Instead He chose to give us free will whereby we ourselves play a part in the Redemption. We accept Him or refuse Him accordingly as we freely open or close the inside latch on the door of our heart.

Unto His own He comes this Christmas just as He came the first night when the angels' voices broke out in song over the hills of Bethlehem. Whether he finds a place in the inn of our beings or not remains our decision to make. We are the innkeepers to have and to hold, or to turn Him away and hear recorded once again those tragic, terrifying words, "And His own received Him not."[63]

---

[63] John 1:11.

Walking down a prominent avenue in a great city during the Advent days just preceding Christmas, and enjoying the sights of the decorations, the holly and wreaths and festive cheer, a priest was looking particularly for scenes descriptive of the real spirit of the season. His eye was attracted to a beautiful Madonna and Child. It was set off by a splendid display of rich ornamentation. This was seen in a jewelry shop of Fifth Avenue in New York City, and before the Mother and Babe was a long golden chain and cross, evidently of very great value. Adjacent to this were many articles of shining brilliance. And then a card neatly drawn with these words: "Jewelry has always been considered the supreme gift."

It was a beautiful display magnificently appointed and quite dramatically arranged. Perhaps, that is the reason why it left the viewer in a mood for thought. The priest could not help but think quite at variance with the inscription: "Jewelry . . . the _supreme_ gift."

With all due regard to the creative mind of the artist who displayed his wares and so beautifully arranged the setting with Mother and Child, with proper acknowledgment, too, that we usually measure our affection by the priceless gift we present—yet, this phrase misses the mark horribly. The supreme gift is not to be found in silver or gold. The supreme gift is not in anything crafted by human hands.

The supreme gift is not to be discovered in anything this world prizes. The supreme gift is Christ Himself—the Incarnate God, the Eucharistic Presence—"Greater love no man hath. . . ."[64] The supreme gift is the one God gave to us over 1900 years ago, and He continues to give to us today in His Eucharistic life upon our altars.

The "supreme gift" comes from above: "Pour out ye heavens the dew from above and let the clouds rain the just one."[65] The supreme gift is love of God and of neighbor.[66] Upon this depend all other gifts. If I have the goods of earth I can purchase the jewels of time. But not all the world's money can purchase pure love where it does not exist. In this sense the God-fearing laborer is richer than the kings of earth with cold hearts—Mary and Joseph are richer than all the Herods and Pilates who wear uneasy crowns.

Do we ever stop to think how little pure love of God there is in the world? By pure love of God we mean loving Him for His own sake! When we are motivated by fear of losing heaven and deserving hell, we are moved by selfish interests rather than divine love.[67] This is love worthy of redemption, but it is not the highest type of love.

---

[64] John 15:13.

[65] Isaiah 45:8.

[66] Deuteronomy 6:5.

[67] Although perfect contrition is a far better thing, the fear of

When we pray to Mary, Help of Christians and Mother of Christ, we are often flying to her patronage because we know she can help us from our difficulty. Were we to seek her company and intercessory aid even in time of joy and contentment, then, indeed, we could count ourselves as true children of Mary and lovers of her Son.

Christmas is the season of contrast. God gives His all to us. We bargain with Him. Could we not hold on just a little to the jewels of earth, we ask? They seem so priceless, so supreme! These jewels may be silver, they may be gold, or they may be a thousand different things! But to all of us they represent the difference between accepting Christ or compromising Him. "Unto His own He came and . . ." we are writing the remaining lines deep down in the secret recesses of our hearts. What are we writing? Do we too finish that line with "and they received Him not?" How are we living? We know that St. John tells us, "His own received Him not!" God, have mercy on us—grant us the grace to write in our hearts, "and they received Him!"

---

losing heaven and deserving hell, known as imperfect contrition, nevertheless is sufficient to save one's soul. Man is called to more than that, but this state of imperfect contrition is not, strictly speaking, an impediment but an aid to a soul's quest for eternal happiness, acting as sufficient sorrow to have the soul validly absolved of her sins through the sacrament of confession (see *CCC* 1453).

Christ knocks! The latch is on the inside! Only beings with free will, such as we, can open the door to the inn of our hearts—and if we do, our joy is hundredfold!

Prayer

Jesus, Mary, Joseph, come take rest in the Inn of my heart.

Hewn out of the rock of my daily living, it offers but little shelter.

Kings and queens of earth would never find time for the monotony of my thoughts, nor would they company themselves with such lowliness as my heart offers.

Yet, You, all-holy three, are willing to dwell with me.

Joseph, humble man of carpentry, teach me to accept God's holy will.

Mary, mother of Christ, show yourself a mother to me.

Jesus, Babe of Bethlehem, come into my soul Eucharistically.

Do You, all-holy three, come, possess
my heart, give peace to earth, good will
to men!

Wednesday of the Fourth Week of Advent: Peace on Earth

"And suddenly there was with the angel a multitude of the heavenly army, praising God, and saying: 'Glory to God in the highest; and on earth, peace to men of good will.'"[68]

Peace is more than simply the absence of conflict.

Peace means God's life in our souls. Peace means grace abundant in the souls of men. And so, dismayed by the horrors of war, the suffering and distraught peoples of the globe look to the leaders of the nations for an end, a respite even, from the pain and death of war. On all sides, from friend and foe, from ally and enemy, this desire for a cessation of armed strife comes. But only upon the teachings of the humble Nazarene, who came to earth as a Babe born in a stable, can there be built a lasting order of justice and charity, the two essential notes for a lasting peace.

From Bethlehem's hills will echo the bells of a new Christmastide, announcing anew tidings of joy and the

---

[68] Luke 2:14.

good news of the Gospel to all who will permit such hallowed sounds to filter through the din of the world's excitement and the roar of cannon and shell. From the hill of the Vatican round the world will go the echo of Christ in the voice of His Vicar. Yet, error and prejudice and hatred will blind many hearts and dull many souls to that message of the Pope of Peace.[69] Still our priests and bishops pray, "O God, from whom all just works do proceed, give to Your servants that peace which the world cannot give, that our hearts may be disposed to obey Your commandments and that our days may be peaceful."[70]

The Pope's peace plan includes the right of nations to independence, disarmament, a world court where universal justice for small nations may be obtained, and principally a return to God and religion.[71] Shortly after the accession of Pope Pius XII to the papal throne in March of 1939, war broke out in Europe in September of the same year. Yet, he has more than any other man living sought

---

[69] When this was written in 1953, Pope Pius XII labored immensely to bring about peace in this world, as shown in his motto "Opus Justitiae Pax," "The work of justice shall be peace" (Isaiah 32:17). Pope Pius worked for years to bring about peace between European nations from his election in 1939 throughout World War II and the Cold War of the 1950s.

[70] Collect from the Votive Mass for Peace.

[71] These goals were termed "Pope Pius' Five Point Peace Plan."

daily by virtue of his office to avert the spread of that global catastrophe. "Nothing is gained by war that cannot be achieved by peace," he has warned the nations. How true the words have been and how sorrowful have the nations become through loss of their choicest citizens because they have not heeded his advice.

The Holy Father has spoken many times of peace at Christmas. How true his words but recently uttered—"a true peace is not the mathematical result of a proportion of forces, but in its last and deepest meaning is a moral and juridical process. It is not, in fact, achieved without employment of force, and its very existence needs the support of a normal measure of power. But the real function of this force, if it is to be morally correct, should consist in protecting and defending and not in lessening or suppressing rights. An hour like the present—so full of possibilities for vast beneficent progress no less than for fatal defects and blunders—has perhaps never been seen in the history of mankind."

Today, the believing world, though rent asunder by the heresy of different beliefs, turns to Bethlehem. Catholics blessed with the divine deposit of faith that has remained unchanged through the ages turn to the crib of the tabernacle and the Babe of the Eucharist and, bending low in adoration like the shepherds of old, cry out "Emmanuel"—God with us. There in the picture of faith and devotion is the humble Mary and her spouse Joseph, true to the divine summons watching over the child of peace.

Though there may be no peace in the world where bombers fly overhead and munition plants keep wheeling out supplies, yet there will be millions of hearts and souls attuned to the divine will of God. These souls who practice justice and charity in the little world of their souls will have the blessings of peace, the peace which the world cannot give: the knowledge of a good conscience and the assurance that God is watching over their eternal destiny and protecting their souls from evil. In such hearts Bethlehem's message "Glory to God and peace to men of good will" will find a hallowed place.

Prayer

O Lord, inspire rulers and peoples with counsels of meekness. Heal the discord that tears nations asunder and bring true peace, Your peace. You, who shed Your precious blood that men might live as brothers, bring them all once more together in peace, that the Peace of Christ may ever reign in our hearts, families, and nations. You who live and reign with the Father in the unity of the Holy Spirit, God, forever and ever. Amen.

Thursday of the Fourth Week of Advent: Christmas Means Charity—Heaven's First Law

Love is the greatest power in the world, stronger even than death.[72] It depends not upon coercion or force but upon inspiration. Love, which is charity, is the first law of God. Indeed, all other laws are rooted in it. Love depends not upon any power in the world but has its roots and inspiration in God. Only the almighty power of God is capable of inspiring divine love from which all human love flows, and without divine inspiration love cannot endure.

Like the very flower that the lover bestows upon his loved one—the rose, which bears many thorns—so true love is often born out of sorrow. Charity, then, which is love of God and of neighbor, shares joy and sorrow alike.

These considerations should prompt us to make an intention in all that we do for our neighbors. That intention should be purified each day with prayer, and that should be a prayer that all things we do might be prompted by love of God. No human motive, no matter how noble, can take the place of charity. No philanthropic project, no matter how stupendous, if not properly rooted in God as well

---

[72] Song of Songs 8:6.

as man, can be compared to the widow's mite prompted by the inspiration divine. In these days when so many fundraising drives are being carried on to alleviate the sufferings of peoples both here and abroad, it is well to remember prayerfully the words of the Apostle on charity: that it will avail nothing unless God is part of our plans.[73]

If the Vicar of Christ had a thousand voices he could enunciate a thousand different heart-stirring appeals, he could speak of the neediest cases, and stir thousands of hearts to pity and urge them to sacrifice. Yet, all the thousand voices and all their neediest cases would have but one motivation and one inspiration: God. For all that we do for neighbor, we do out of the motive of love of God. This is charity!

Did you ever playfully, but never with more serious intent, ask a little child the question: "How much do you love me?" Then did you think long and meditatively on the child's answer? Do you remember that there were no

---

[73] 1 Corinthians 13:1–3: "If I speak with the tongues of men, and of angels, and have not charity, I am become as sounding brass, or a tinkling cymbal. And if I should have prophecy and should know all mysteries, and all knowledge, and if I should have all faith, so that I could remove mountains, and have not charity, I am nothing. And if I should distribute all my goods to feed the poor, and if I should deliver my body to be burned, and have not charity, it profiteth me nothing."

words spoken? There was only an eloquent gesture. Little arms were outstretched all the way as far as they could. The child was showing that its love was boundless. Now, perhaps, if one could phrase the same question to Jesus as one knelt before the crib at Christmas or the crucifix on Good Friday, "How much, O Lord, do You love me?" he would obtain the same answer. The answer would be identical to the little child's response—no words spoken, but an eloquent gesture of arms outstretched all the way in token of His boundless love.

If we are attuned to the charity of the Sacred Heart from whence all love that is lasting must flow, then we will practice the perfect way of life and live according to the first law of love.

Prayer

Bless, O Lord, all our hearts today and move them to pity. Let this pity be for themselves, lest one day they appear before You naked of the riches of charity. Being moved to compunction for our sins we shall then love You more and show this love to men. You who live and reign with the Father in the unity of the Holy Spirit, God, forever and ever. Amen.

Friday of the Fourth Week of Advent: A Sign in the Heavens

When the autumnal skies show forth the northern lights or Aurora Borealis, it is a wonderful sight to behold. If, however, one is not aware of what causes this phenomenon of nature, there may be fear and trepidation of heart.

In somewhat the same manner did fear enter the hearts of the shepherds on the first Christmas night, for they were deeply frightened: "And behold an angel of the Lord stood by them and the glory of God shone round them, and they feared exceedingly." But their fear quickly gave way to wonder and joy once they knew why the angelic messenger appeared: "And the angel said to them, 'Do not be afraid, for behold, I bring you good news of great joy which shall be to all the people; for there has been born to you today in the town of David a Savior, who is Christ the Lord. And this shall be a sign to you; you will find an infant wrapped in swaddling clothes and lying in a manger.'"[74]

Their fear was a natural thing, but their hearts were good. They listened to God's angels. Inspiration took hold of their hearts and grace took root in their souls. Their fears were gone as they said: "Let us go over to Bethlehem

---

[74] Luke 2:9–12.

and see this thing that has come to pass, which the Lord has made known to us.

"So they went in haste, and they found Mary and Joseph, and the Babe lying in the manger. And when they had seen, they understood what had been told them concerning this Child. And all who heard marveled at the things told them by the shepherds . . . and the shepherds returned, glorifying and praising God for all that they had heard and seen, even as it was spoken to them."[75]

In a world threatened by war that can produce catastrophes on an unprecedented scale, each one of us has reason to fear. Temptation lurks on every side. Godlessness and distrust of fellow man, caused by prejudice and hatred which are the weapons of a materialistic order, run rampant. A lack of moral restraint is responsible for many of our present woes. Man has forgotten God. Fear is everywhere.

We are the shepherds of this modern world as we prepare these Advent days for the coming of Christmas. Our fears can be sanctified if we act like the shepherds of old. They listened. Then went in haste once they received divine direction. They found Christ with Mary and Joseph. They

---

[75] Luke 2:15–18, 20.

told others of His presence, who marveled at the things told by the shepherds. They glorified and praised God.

Many people are possessed of fears. The signs in the heavens of man-made explosions make them shake lest the earth be destroyed and mankind ravaged.

But there are also other signs in the heavens—God, too, has signs. "And a great sign appeared in heaven: a woman clothed with the sun, and the moon was under her feet, and upon her head a crown of twelve stars."[76]

There is something about the darkness of the night that causes grave fears in many hearts. Perhaps, it is because we get down deep into our own consciences at night. In broad daylight we can distract our souls. At night we are aware of the murmurings of our hearts. We are alone and with God. But there are too many hearts that seek to be apart from God. They torture themselves with goals and ambitions that have roots only in this world. They let passion rule their plans when divine love should be the architect of their dreams. They are face to face with the disaster of living for self and the unhappiness of hearts which refuse the companionship of the saints.

And, yet, the darkness of the night can be full of the wonder of God. Nature speaks and softly chants a hymn

---

[76] Apocalypse 12:1.

of praise to the Creator. The stars look down and tell us of His ever-present eyes. The moon reminds us of the Lady who defeated the dragon of evil. A soul straight with God is never fearful of the darkness, for he is sure that he will awaken to the Light of the world.

Beautiful to behold is the modern-day planetarium where one may see a replica of the heavens. Here one can behold the sun sinking in the western sky. Then comes darkness, and all at once above the heads of the audience, the whole firmament appears: the Great Bear, the Pleiades, Orion. The moon rises and passes across the sky in calm dignity. Then the planets appear and run their elliptical course. The entrancing sight calls forth expressions of wonderment from the spectators as they seem to sense in awe the hand of the omnipotent Artist and Creator of the universe.

As one leaves the Planetarium and pushes his way through the crowd he is suddenly jolted back to earth. All too frequently this great occasion for grace, this moment of the consciousness of God in the heavens is crushed and some human consideration takes its place. What should have been the beginning of wonder leading us to prayer and reflection is aborted and our minds, which were made for the contemplation of the things of God, return to mundane matters.

The night can be full of wonder and hope when, like the shepherds, we watch and pray. The stars can lead us to God, if we turn out the lights of the world and give the Holy Spirit a chance to move our beings.

Christmas can be full of the fear of the Lord and the beginning of wisdom or it can be replete with worldly forebodings. Like the shepherds, we must have our fears assuaged only by God.

Prayer

Blessed Savior of men, teach us the lesson of the Shepherds and remind us that the goal of life is not earth but heaven. Guide our eyes to look up to the stars in the heavens and not down to fleeting vanities of earth. Remind us by the sweet promptings of Your grace that we are building a cathedral of the spirit when we turn our fears into prayers. For unless, O Lord, we build with You, we labor in vain. Unless You, O Lord, keep the city of our hearts, we work in vain in keeping it. Help us always to keep our eyes on our celestial homeland, and always strive to be working towards Your eternal halls. You who live and reign with the Father in the unity of the Holy Spirit, God, forever and ever. Amen.

THE CHRISTMAS SEASON

Vigil of the Nativity of the Lord: Prayer and Fasting

God is lavish in His generosity. He has bountifully bestowed upon men and women of this age many beneficent gifts and graces. As such, we are the custodians of His treasures, and He shall exact an account of our stewardship, for to whom much is given, much is expected.[77]

Today, as never before, there are opportunities for rebuilding the world according to the divine plan of things. We are confronted with many problems, but all these grant us opportunities in the form of challenges.

The Church is looking today to Christian homes as the cradles where young hearts may be schooled in the

---

[77] Luke 12:48.

knowledge of God in order that they may renew the face of the earth. It is not so much the gifts of God to which we look, for these are always present, as God is all-bountiful and good. It is the use of these gifts that counts. The proper use of these gifts rests with the servants of God. To use well the gifts of God some shall have to respond to the call to the religious life, other sons and daughters shall have to meet the challenge of a pagan world and go forth as Christian parents to replenish the earth with new love and life and grace.

To those who have no faith there seems to be a great chasm between the state of marriage and the religious life. Yet this is not true! For each state, carrying its own duties and privileges, likewise carries its own joys and satisfactions. Each one of us in every station of life has a vocation, St. Paul assures us.[78] To the crucifix must all men go to learn the true purpose of life, and all must climb the hill of Calvary, where sacrifice saw its perfection, as all who responded to God's grace were lifted up above the earth: Our Lady, St. Mary Magdalene, St. John, and St. Dismas, the Centurion!

Life and love have meaning only in the belief that God is our Father, Jesus Christ our Redeemer, and the Holy

---

[78] See 1 Corinthians 12.

Spirit our Sanctifier. Life shakes off its dull, drab cloak of humdrum monotony only when there is purpose behind our every act, and when each day is consecrated to the end for which God gave it to us.

The surest way to enjoy the gifts of God is to place them at His feet and to give them back to Him and to our neighbors in humble acknowledgment of the fact that we are but custodians of God's treasures. Giving away the gifts of God in fulfillment of the purpose of life is what the mother and father do as they bring life to the world and consecrate their own selves to fashioning more and more God's image in the souls of those entrusted to their care. Giving away the gifts of God is what the priest, the religious do as they devote their talents to the glory of God and the service of men and bring to souls communion with the life of God.

Today, as perhaps never before, we have opportunities to dedicate ourselves to the rebuilding of a new world of the spirit.

God alone is supreme. We are His stewards. May He grant us the grace always to be worthy custodians of His gifts, cheerful dispensers of His bounty, and stewards who need have no fear of rendering an account. What better time to meditate upon making a return of the gifts than Advent when preparing for Christmas!

Prayer

God the Father, Son, and Holy Spirit, hear our prayer, we beseech You, and grant to Your servants that peace of mind and concord of soul that, using well Your gifts and graces, we may be found worthy in Your sight of everlasting reward. You who live and reign with the Father in the unity of the Holy Spirit, God, forever and ever. Amen.

Feast of the Nativity of the Lord: "A Child Is Born"

"There went forth a decree from Caesar Augustus, that the whole world should be enrolled. This enrolling was first made by Cyrinus the governor of Syria, and all went to be enrolled, every one into his own city. And Joseph also went up from Galilee, out of the city of Nazareth into Judea, to the city of David, which is called Bethlehem, because he was of the house and family of David, to be enrolled with Mary his espoused wife, who was with child. And it came to pass, that when they were there, her days were accomplished, that she should be delivered. And she brought forth her first-born son, and wrapped him up in swaddling clothes, and laid him in a manger, because there was no room for them in the inn. And there were in the same country shepherds watching, and keeping the night watches over their flock. And behold, an angel of the Lord stood by them, and the brightness of God shone round about them; and they feared with a great fear. And the angel said unto them: 'Fear not; for, behold, I bring you good tidings of great joy, which shall be to all the people: for this day is born to you a Savior, who is Christ the Lord, in the city of David. And this shall be a sign unto you: You shall find the infant wrapped in swaddling clothes and laid in a manger.' And suddenly there was with the angel a multitude of the heavenly host praising God, and saying: 'Glory to God in the highest; and on earth peace to men of good will.'"[79]

The message of Christmas is the greatest story ever told: "a Child is born to us, and a son is given to us."[80] And that Child is God, born of Mary ever-virgin, a maiden espoused to a man named Joseph, the humble carpenter of Nazareth. The glory of the universe has come unto us through the most extraordinary, humble means.

The message of birth is always an occasion for joy, but what greater joy could there be than the message of the birth of God amongst men! For joy of this birth the angels sang, echoing over the hills of Bethlehem, a *Gloria*

---

[79] Luke 2:1–14.

[80] Isaiah 9:6.

in Excelsis Deo, and the message: "For this day is born to you a Savior, who is Christ the Lord, in the city of David. And this shall be a sign unto you: You shall find the Infant wrapped in swaddling clothes and laid in a manger." In the *Introit* of the third Christmas Mass[81] we read: "A Child is born to us, and a son is given to us." The Christ Child is born for our salvation. He is the Son of God! He is given to us—what a gift at Christmas!

Recently I spoke to a little six-year-old school child whom I saw standing outside the school building shortly after 9 o'clock. She was in great fear lest if she entered the school—for she was late—she would incur severe penalties from her teacher. I offered to take her into the classroom to plead her cause, for she was in tears. But she refused to let me do so and decided to return home again to her parents. I imagine there was nothing so terrible at that particular moment for that little girl than to face her teacher. Although we may laugh at this, we must see that we often are very much the same. It is not with a teacher, but often it can be with the confessional, or rather, with the

---

[81] In the pre-conciliar Mass, the *Vetus Ordo*, there are three different Masses with different readings on Christmas Day : Midnight Mass, the Mass at Dawn, and the Mass in the Day. The post-conciliar Mass, the *Novus Ordo*, does not distinguish readings for various points of the feast day.

great God of heaven and earth. Our troubles at Christmas time in a war-ridden world are more tumultuous to us than the raging seas, but I wonder if God does not see another side. You may say, what could be more grave than the suicidal act of war, brother killing brother? Does God ridicule our ills, our prayers as petty and worthless by letting this onslaught of bloodshed continue? No! But God can see the ultimate end of it all—that good shall triumph after the world has been scourged at the pillar of suffering and has crucified its own pride and sensuality. For we are but children to God; yes, children of a larger growth, and what matters it all if we are purged of our selfishness, our waywardness, our sinfulness here, so long as we gain the victory over our lower impulses and win life eternal?

Could nature talk to us on a beautiful night as the stars twinkle in the heavens and bombers block out momentarily the light of the moon, she would say to us, that which is small in you, you are magnifying, and that which is great in you, you are minimizing. Your destiny lies beyond the stars, beyond the moon, beyond the earth. Your short span of earthly existence is so unimportant as compared with your eternal destiny that you are foolish to take anything serious in life except the saving of your immortal soul. If the oxen in the cave of Bethlehem could only speak, these beasts of burden would tell us that we would find Christ in a humble cave of the Holy Family and not in the inn of the world. If nature, against whose starry background the bombers fly and upon whose bosom of the sea the ships and submarines sport in war, could but utter a word, all the elements of creation would all sing, "Glory to God!" and lament "Oh, pitiful man! How foolish are you who war in frenzied hate!"

Ah, but the skies do speak, the stars speak! Yes, and the oceans speak! They tell us of God: of His power, His might, His beauty, His omnipotence! For those who have faith the handwriting of God is seen in everything He has written, be it carved in the rocks, the brooks, the sky, or the sea! "I see His blood upon the rose . . . His face in every flower," said Joseph Plunkett.[82]

Look into the face of a child this Christmas, and you will see there the hope of the future world. All your cares will have ceased a thousand times over when that child reaches maturity. Look into the face of the Child in the crib, the virgin Mother, and Joseph, and you will find the message of Christmas. Lift up your heart, as the priest at Mass reads: "A Child is born," and sing "Glory to God in the highest, and on earth, peace to men of good will."

---

[82] "I See His Blood upon the Rose," by Joseph Mary Plunkett.

Prayer

Babe of Bethlehem, help me to minimize my worldly ills by placing them all at Your feet and help me to magnify in true perspective the Church's teaching that nothing counts so much as a good life. Help me to be humble by placing all success at Your feet, that I may know true greatness consists in acknowledging that all I have is Yours, and You are mine, and I am the littlest child of God. You who live and reign with the Father in the unity of the Holy Spirit, God, forever and ever. Amen.

The Feast of the Epiphany of the Lord: Gifts for God

"When Jesus therefore was born in Bethlehem of Juda, in the days of King Herod, behold, there came wise men from the East to Jerusalem, saying: 'Where is he that is born king of the Jews? For we have seen his star in the East, and are come to adore him.' And King Herod hearing this, was troubled, and all Jerusalem with him. . . . Then Herod privately calling the wise men, learned diligently of them the time of the star which appeared to them. And sending them into Bethlehem, said: 'Go and diligently inquire after the child, and when you have found him, bring me word again, that I also may come and adore him.' Who having heard the king, went their way; and behold the star which they had seen in the East, went before them, until it came and stood over where the child was. And seeing the star they rejoiced with exceeding great joy. And entering the house, they found the child with Mary his mother, and falling down they adored him: and opening their treasures, they offered him gifts: gold, frankincense, and myrrh. And having received an answer in sleep that they should not return to Herod, they went back another way into their country."[83]

The Magi were real kings, as was Herod. The contrast between the two, however, is vast. The Magi are known as angelic men, venerated as saints best known for bowing down before the Christ Child; Herod is known as a diabolical man, best known for cutting down children in an attempt to maintain his throne. The Magi worshiped the only true King, God. Herod worshiped himself. The Magi gave their gifts to God. Herod was seeking God's gifts for man.

To every soul God gives certain gifts, talents, and opportunities for heavenly grace. When we use God's gifts for His greater honor and glory we bring joy to our own

---

[83] Matthew 2:1–12.

hearts and peace of soul. The gifts of God are stolen when we use them for ourselves. Peace to men of good will can come only when men imitate the Magi and not Herod.

The Feast of the Epiphany is the day of the manifestation of God to the Gentiles. To shepherds and kings He manifested His glory, the glory of the only-begotten Son of God. Herod had an opportunity as did the Magi, but his heart was wicked from the deeds of a profligate life. He was a murderer at heart. He proved how wicked he was when in his anger he slew all the male children in and around Bethlehem who were two years old or under.

The deeds of the Magi, who were really kings at heart, for they worshiped the King of the universe, have lived down through the years in honor and dignity. The evil machinations of Herod died in ignominy. When Herod was dead, and let us remember that there comes a day when all wicked tyrants die, an angel of the Lord appeared in a dream to Joseph in Egypt, saying, "Arise, and take the child and his mother, and go into the land of Israel, for those who sought the child's life are dead."[84]

Our deeds, if inspired of God, will live on to attest to our faith and virtue. God has blessed us with kingly hopes and heavenly grace. Like the Magi of old we must turn

---

[84] Matthew 2:20.

aside from the wicked promptings of unprincipled men to find a new pathway of virtue that leads to the feet of God. Gifts we have been given. Talents have been bestowed upon us. Our paths must necessarily cross with the ways of the wicked, but our hearts and souls must always be attuned to God's angels of grace, lest we be confused by pseudo-kings who promise us an earthly paradise. Such when thwarted will always act like Herod and make innocent blood flow as they destroy the bodies of men.

God manifests Himself to us in many different ways. The path of virtue is usually lit by a star. That star may be a good parent who raises us in piety; it could be a priest who directs our soul in virtue; it could be a sickness or tragedy which brings us to our knees, physically or spiritually, in imitation of Him who fell on the way of the cross. Whatever be the star, it will shine the brighter if we pray for gifts that we may sanctify by our lives and lay at the feet of the King.

Unto each is given a vocation in life. It is God's call to a particular state wherein we may the better sanctify our souls and lead others to Him. Kings we are, all of us, when God bestows the great grace that sanctifies. Gold can be used to pave the way to God; frankincense can be utilized to give God the sweetness of our Christian action and virtuous life; myrrh and life's sorrows can make us more like unto the thorn-crowned King. But all the joys and sorrows of life are the gifts of God. They must never be used as Herod used them to bring devastation to hearts. Each one of the gifts can be used for our own selfish motives, and not for the glory of God. Gold is abused when used apart from God. Frankincense can lead to sin when poured out upon creatures apart from the Creator. Myrrh, life's sorrows, can be bitter when seen apart from God and the crucifix. We must recall that every gift which we possess is a gift from God to help us return to Him; each gift must be raised up, immolated like the bread and the wine of Mass to bring us into communion with God, raising the dignity of the gift and the giver by bringing them in closer imitation of their Creator.

The star of the heavens is meant for kings to follow. We have kingly hearts since they have been redeemed by the blood of the Savior. That star must be followed even when we have to circumvent the false kings of earth who promise an earthly reward. We must seek God and spurn Herod, lest the blood of innocents again be made to sprinkle a crimson carpet over the beautiful verdant earth where the children of God walk.

Prayer

O Jesus, infinite Savior, teach us to use the gifts of life and love for Him who is the Life of the world and love eternal. Give us the guidance and direction of the stars of heaven in the example of the saints and Our Lady, that we may not attend to the false example of wicked men who shed innocent blood. As we go to an altar where the bread and wine are changed into Your body and blood, so may we go daily with all of Your gifts, that we may sanctify our lives with the gold of Your love, the frankincense of prayer, and the myrrh of our sorrows that shall be turned into the joys of eternal life at the throne of the King of kings in heaven. You who live and reign with the Father in the unity of the Holy Spirit, God, forever and ever. Amen.